Other Titles in the Smart Pop Series

Taking the Red Pill

Seven Seasons of Buffy

Five Seasons of Angel

What Would Sipowicz Do?

Stepping through the Stargate

The Anthology at the End of the Universe

Finding Serenity

The War of the Worlds

Alias Assumed

Navigating the Golden Compass

Farscape Forever!

Flirting with Pride and Prejudice

Revisiting Narnia

Totally Charmed

King Kong Is Back!

Mapping the World of Harry Potter

The Psychology of The Simpsons

The Unauthorized X-Men

The Man from Krypton

Welcome to Wisteria Lane

Star Wars on Trial

The Battle for Azeroth

Boarding the Enterprise

Getting Lost

James Bond in the 21st Century

So Say We All

Investigating CSI

Literary Cash

Webslinger

HALO EFFECT

An Unauthorized Look at the Most Successful Video Game of All Time

EDITED BY

GLENN YEFFETH

with Jennifer Thomason

Special thanks to Daniel Finnegan Barbour
for his valuable comments and feedback.

BENBELLA BOOKS, INC.
Dallas, Texas

BENBELLA

BenBella Books, Inc.
6440 N. Central Expressway, Suite 617
Dallas, TX 75206
www.benbellabooks.com
Send feedback to feedback@benbellabooks.com

Printed in the United States of America
10 9 8 7 6 5 4 3 2 1

Library of Congress Cataloging-in-Publication Data

Halo effect : the unauthorized look at the most successful video game of all time / edited by Glenn Yeffeth with Jennifer Thomason.
    p. cm.
  ISBN 1-933771-11-9
  1. Video games. I. Yeffeth, Glenn, 1961– II. Thomason, Jennifer.
  GV1469.37.H35 2007
  794.8—dc22

                                                                            2006039329

Proofreading by Erica Lovett and Jennifer Thomason
Printed by Bang Printing
Cover design by Mondolithic Studios, Inc.
Text design and composition by John Reinhardt Book Design

Distributed by Independent Publishers Group
To order call (800) 888-4741
www.ipgbook.com

For special sales contact Yara Abuata at yara@benbellabooks.com

To Margaret, who means even more to me than Halo.

CONTENTS

Matthew Woodring Stover

YOU ARE THE MASTER CHIEF

The Master Chief is a cold-hearted killing machine.
So why do we care about him?

THE GREAT-TIMES-FORTY GRANDPAPPY of MilSef—that's military science fiction, for any n00bs out there—wrote his fantastical epic with a clear intention of not just telling a story, but celebrating the enduring virtues of his warrior culture... because for him (kinda like us, for better or worse), the great warrior was the exemplar of everything that was admirable in humanity—and pretty much everything less than admirable, too. Sometimes even in the same guy. War is the crucible of character.

War by its nature reveals, in a very real sense, capital-T Truth.

Whether he was right about this is beyond the scope of this essay; let's just say that no less an authority on human nature than Shakespeare would agree (*q.v: The Second Part of Henry the Fourth, The Tragedy of King Richard II, The History of Troilus and Cressida*), and even a cynic like Nietzsche used the aforementioned fantastical epic as evidence of the enduring lure of human cruelty and the inescapable drive that he called "the will to power."

This grandpappy was, as devoted readers might have already guessed, Homer (and not Simpson, either), and the fantastical epic in question is

The Iliad. Why the hell am I yammering about *The Iliad* in an essay devoted to the Halo franchise?

Because fundamentally, they're the same thing. Different faces of the same coin.

Yes, they are, and if you'll stick with me for a few pages I'll not only show you what I'm talking about, but explain why you should give a damn.

First, my standard disclaimer: I am a notorious crank. I am also narrow-minded, arbitrary, and cantankerous. It would be best for all of us if, while you read the following, you remember that the BenBella folks *already knew that* when they asked me to contribute to this book. So don't come crying to me. I'm entirely *their* fault.

Second: I'm not much of a console gamer. There are only a handful of Xbox games I've ever played, and I don't even own a Playstation, a Gamecube, or any of the rest of that crap. I don't have *time* to play games, dammit—I have *contracts* due! The only game console I own is the aforementioned Xbox, and I own that for one reason only, which falls under "Third."

Third: I bought my Xbox so I can play *Halo: Combat Evolved.*

Would I lie to you?

A friend of mine who *is* a major-league console gamer got me to try it—your basic crack-dealer tactic, y'know, the first hit's free—and I was done for.

Being who I am, though (cf. *notorious crank*, above), I can't make myself be entirely content to just let the game be the game. I started to think of the game in terms of its *story*, not its gameplay, partly because the story is superbly plotted (in its own straightforward way) and partly because writing stories along the same lines—Lone Superhero vs. Impossible Odds—is more or less my specialty.

Okay: here comes the dry bit.

Devoted followers of the Smart Pop series will likely already know that I spend a lot of time whinging on about the specific *meta-thematic intention* of the various genres and sub-genres. By that I mean the thematic concerns that essentially define any serious-minded story written in that genre. Romance stories are defined by *the search for love.* Detective stories are defined by *the search for truth.* Cop stories are defined by *going to get the bad guys.* The soap opera (or its proper name, Kitchen Sink Drama) is defined by *the struggle of everyday life.*

The primary meta-theme of the war story was laid out by ol' Homer almost 3,000 years ago: *war is the crucible of character.*

In most, if not all, serious war stories, the state of war is (explicitly or metaphorically) identified with the characters' whole world—with, one might say, existence itself. Existence itself might be utterly indifferent, and understanding this marks your transition from child to adult; then you have Crane's *The Red Badge of Courage.* Existence might be ridiculously hostile; that's Heller's *Catch-22.* Existence might be so essentially futile that the only answer is love; Vonnegut's *Slaughterhouse Five.*

Further, the protagonist of a war story is implicitly identified with either our aspirations toward nobility and heroism (*Le Chanson de Roland, To Hell and Back, Guadalcanal Diary*), or our fears that these aspirations are only a trap for the naïve (Trumbo's *Johnny Got His Gun,* Haldeman's *The Forever War* without the tacked-on happy ending, Remarque's *All Quiet on the Western Front*).

MilSef (along with its little brother, military fantasy) occupies a special position in the genre; it is the only sub-genre of the war story in which every element of the story is entirely under the author's control. The nature of the conflict, the ground, the weapons, the style of engagement, the odds, the politics, *everything.* The author can (and should) tailor each and every smallest detail to suit his or her point of view; there is no historical necessity (i.e., "Well, it *has* to be this way—it's how Napoleon actually deployed his troops!" or whatever). The author can't appeal to historical or technical fact as an excuse for a plot point or story element (unless he or she is working in some sub-sub-sub-genre like steampunk or historical fantasy, which are more-or-less special cases; we'll leave those out, as they're each worth whole essays of their own).

And MilSef adds another thematic element to the war story stew (one of the meta-themes of SF itself, inescapable in any SF that includes non-human characters of any description): *What does it mean to be human?*

This brings us back to the Master Chief. What do we know about him?

Just how human *is* Our Favorite Bad-ass Cyborg?

Let's see: we know he was constructed—well, *cybernetically modified*—on Reach, the most heavily defended outpost of the human race, as part of the SPARTAN-II project. With his cybernetic implants, he is larger, stronger, faster, and more deadly than any human alive. His integrated MJOLNIR battle armor relieves him of the need to breathe, eat, drink, or rest. He slaughters prodigious numbers of heavily armed enemies without fear, hesitation, or psychological consequence. He doesn't even seem to have a conscience or any wisp of empathy; witnessing the slaughter of his Marine companions doesn't even rate a comment. He is a remorseless killing machine, entirely goal-directed, incapable of even second thoughts. His only distinctly human characteristic is a mordantly deadpan sense of humor.

He is, in fact, a great deal less human than the *explicitly non-human* artificial intelligence Cortana, riding along in his battle-armor's neural net; she, at least, shows sadness at the death of Marines and flashes of anger (notably at 343 Guilty Spark), along with sarcastic wit and obvious concern with both her own survival and that of the human race.

The Master Chief, by contrast, is concerned only with accomplishing his mission.

It seems pretty clear that the Master Chief represents the first type of fictive war hero: the one who, like Roland at Roncevalles or Horatius at the Bridge, represents our aspirations toward the Noble Virtues—y'know, personal courage, devotion to duty, indomitable will, self-sacrifice, and martial skill. All that *parfit gentil knight of renown* crap. There is never the slightest suggestion of human frailty in his character.

Eric Nylund, in his novelization, assures us that the Master Chief's first name is John, which I presume is a bit of an in-joke: a product of the SPARTAN project named John? "John Spartan" is the name of Sylvester Stallone's character in the film *Demolition Man*. Why do I suspect this is more than a coincidence? Because Sylvester Stallone also played another character named John, who is somewhat more directly related to the Master Chief—who is, in fact, a direct ancestor.

I'm talking, of course, about John Rambo.

Don't see the connection?

Like the Master Chief, Rambo is a super-soldier, created by a government program (in his case, Special Forces training), who exists in a perpetual state of war. It's all he's good at; it's all he does. When he's not being used to beat the crap out of the Bad Guys, he has to be sequestered from society (for Rambo, in prison or in a remote monastery in Thailand; for the Master Chief, it's cold storage). Rambo, like the Master Chief, is the ultimate Army of One; he fights single-handedly against impossible odds and he *always wins in the end*.

What's interesting about Rambo, in this context, is how clearly the films depict the extreme price he pays for being a superhuman killing machine (well, except *Rambo III*, which—like *Star Trek V* and the anesthetic sequels to *The Matrix*—is best left in the Dustbin of Hollywood's Crap Ideas). The original *First Blood* is, in fact, explicitly *about* this damage; John Rambo is depicted as an emotionally shattered loner, alienated and violent, a prisoner of extreme training and post-traumatic stress disorder. The state of war is the only place he feels at home.

The Master Chief doesn't suffer from this problem. First, there is no peace-time society, not for him, and second, he doesn't seem to have any emotions to damage. He is as indestructible emotionally as he is physically.

In this, he is clearly more the descendant of another fictional super-hero, Captain America. Ever since his debut in *Captain America* No. 1, way back in March 1941, Cap has been the exemplar of those Noble Virtues I was listing above. Not to mention that he, too, is a government-created super-soldier.

But a funny thing has happened to Captain America since he was found frozen in that ice floe in *Avengers* No. 4: not only does he have a conscience (that has often led him to question or outright defy the American government), but he was clearly tormented by the "deaths" of his young partner, Bucky Barnes, and his one-time lover, SHIELD agent Sharon Carter. He has become, in his later incarnation, much more troubled and thoughtful; it's been a trademark of his adventures since the 1970s that his ideals are often in direct conflict with the necessities of his situation.

Then there's the real-life Captain America, Audie Murphy.

Just like Steve Rogers, Audie Murphy was a scrawny, sickly kid who was turned down by the American armed forces in WWII (twice, in fact: by the Marines and by the Navy), and who after finally being accepted became the closest thing to a real-life super-soldier this country's ever seen; he's still the most-decorated soldier in the history of the U.S. Army. He also spent his post-war life suffering from insomnia, depression, drug addiction, chronic nightmares, and other symptoms of post-traumatic stress disorder; it's said that sometimes he couldn't sleep unless he had a gun under his pillow. Ever the hero, he went public with his condition and became an outspoken advocate for the extension of veteran's benefits to cover treatment for combat-related mental illness.

Audie Murphy's story is a real-life bridge between the WWII-era fiction of *Captain America* and the post-Vietnam fiction of John Rambo; he doesn't let us forget the harsh reality that underlies military heroics.

Can you imagine the Master Chief having post-traumatic stress disorder?

Of course not. He's not *designed* for it.

Which is, I think, the point.

Sure, there's a supra-narrative reason for this; how much fun would the bloody game be if you had to spend most of your time shivering in a corner, waiting for the bad guys to come and kill you? Hell, you might as well play *Call of Cthulhu*. But I'm not talking game mechanics, here. I'm talking *story*.

Halo: Combat Evolved is pure MilSef; every detail is under the control of the creators. They could have made the Master Chief every bit as human as they wanted him to be. In fact, I'm pretty sure that this is exactly what they did.

He's every bit as human as they want him to be.

So, now we have to ask a slightly scary question: *why* did they make him so thoroughly un-human?

There's an easy answer to this question: that it's purely marketing strategy, your basic sado-masochistic power-fantasy, directed at all the socially maladroit dweebs out there. A killing machine without weakness or flaw. . . .

The problem with this easy answer is that it is, like most easy answers, just plain wrong.

If you want to be a killing machine without weakness or flaw, you can just go play *Doom*, right? The shooter of *Doom* is ostensibly a great deal more human than the Master Chief, but even after playing through *Doom III* twice, I can't remember the bastard's name. He doesn't have personality. He's a character without *character*. Hell, I've played *Quake*, and *Duke Nuke'em*, and I don't know how many other FPS games, and none of those characters stick in my mind at all; the only one who comes close is (the third-person) Sam Fisher from the *Splinter Cell* trilogy—and Peter Jackson ain't makin' a movie about *him*. . . .

Remember, we're talking MilSef here. If they wanted a flawless killing machine, they could have *made* him a machine. But they didn't. Machines cannot be heroes. A machine is fearless not because of courage, but because it is incapable of feeling fear. Of feeling anything at all.

But *you* can feel. You can feel fear, albeit second hand, when the Master Chief is cornered by unbeatable odds. You can feel pride in the skill you've developed with his weapons. You can feel elation at whipping Covenant ass and a thrill every time the Grunts spot you, scream, "It's *him*! We're all gonna die!", and run like hell.

That's why he's human. Because you are.

Halo is, remarkably enough, a shining example of post-modernist narrative, even though it hides its post-modernist credentials behind a storm of rock 'n' roll ass-kicking. One of the defining elements of post-modern art is the explicit recognition that the audience—the reader, the viewer, the listener, whatever—is an integral part of the art. That you're not just watching the play, you're *in* it, too; your perception is creating your own personal play (the one in your head) while the external play goes on. I'm sure you can see how a story-based video game like *Halo* is at least arguably a post-modern work of art, despite its conventional narrative structure; the purpose of a shooter is to put *you* in the action. To make you part of the story. Unlike the aforementioned *Doom* and *Call of Cthulhu* and *Band of Brothers* and nearly every other first-person game, *Halo*'s open structure implicitly recognizes that an integral element of the story is some game-geek sitting in front of an Xbox or staring at a computer monitor. And it recognizes, in fact *demands*, that the experience of the game will be different for different players: the differences in your individual skills, the tactics you use to solve each battle, even your path through the game world will make your experience inherently different from that of any other player.

But some things are the same for everybody, and one of those is crucial: you are the Master Chief. This is why we never see the face under the helmet.

In his seminal work *Understanding Comics*, Scott McCloud, the comic creator and esthetic philosopher, points out (correctly) that cartoons grab us precisely because they are unspecific. The more "cartoony" a character is drawn, the easier it is for us to see ourselves in it. What you see of the Master Chief's face is a convex mirror: a reflection of the world around him, a world that is nothing but war. What you don't see is that the face under the mirror is yours.

This is why he's a cyborg, designed for war and serving no purpose save combat. It's why he's not Audie Murphy, or John Rambo, or even Captain America. Because if he were to be too human, we couldn't believe in him.

More important: we wouldn't feel like we *are* him.

Hell, put a couple gazillion dollars worth of twenty-sixth century technology into me, and even *I* could be a friggin' super-soldier. You, I'm guessing, could make it for less.

Probably a *lot* less; I'm old and creaky.

So, Master Chief, now that we've figured out who you are and *why* you are, let's take a brief look at a couple of the clues to what a post-structuralist would call the *meta-narrative* of the story you're starring in.

Let's start with your MJOLNIR Mark V battle-armor (Mark VI in *Halo II*). You don't have to be a student of Sturluson to get this reference; any aficionado of Marvel Comics can tell you that *Mjolnir* is the name of Thor's hammer, the most powerful weapon in all of Germanic/Norse myth, which makes it a curious name for *armor*...until you register that you are frequently referred to as "a Mark V" or "the Mark V" and are never referenced as someone wearing (or even neuro-cybernetically linked to) Mark V armor.

That's because you *are* the weapon.

It's worth noting, too, that Mjolnir (in addition to being able to crush storm giants, slay dragons, and shatter whole mountains with a single blow) is also a *projectile* weapon. That is, it can strike at range, far from its wielder (kind of like you, Master Chief), and no matter how far it's thrown, *it always returns*.

Also kind of like you.

And then, you're the product of the SPARTAN-II project. Well, if you're number II, who's number I?

You are number VI—no, wait. Wrong story.

What the Spartans are known best for (other than pederasty) is the Battle of Thermopylae, where 300 Spartans under King Leonidas (*not* the Jay Ward character from *Tennessee Tuxedo and Friends*, so just shut up about it) brought the entire two-million-man Persian Army under Xerxes I to a screeching halt for three days—and might have stopped the invasion altogether if they hadn't been betrayed. (There were also about 700 Thespians backing up the Spartans, but not many people remember that—I mean, who gives a crap about actors, right?)

The point is that the Spartans became emblematic of the power of personal heroism: outnumbered some 2,000 to one, they did enough damage to the invaders that after losing the naval engagement at Salamis, Xerxes pretty much gave up on the whole invasion.

Okay: so far, we've figured out you're a weapon, flung a great distance, and that you're designed to hold off a vastly superior invasion force even though you're outnumbered thousands to one. With me so far? Good. Here's the kicker: who's the enemy here?

Remember that the game's creators could have chosen any kind of war, for any reason, in any environment that happened to please them. So, what did they pick?

A *holy war*.

And it's not just a holy war—not merely an SF version of *jihad*—because what you're fighting, the enemy that is the greatest threat humanity has ever, or will ever, face, is a coalition of *different species* united by *one single shared element*.

They're *religious fanatics*.

Get it? It's not about one group: not just Arabs, or just Muslims, or al-Qaeda or Shiite militias; not just Christians or Zionists or Marxists. Religious fanaticism in the game (just like in real life) comes in a bewildering variety of shapes and sizes, each with its own set of strengths and weaknesses. And all of them are a profound and immediate danger to our way of life—er, our planet. Yeah, that's it.

The game implicitly characterizes your enemy, Master Chief, as fanaticism itself.

You think this is an accident? At a time when our society—our whole culture—is under attack?

Coincidence seems unlikely.

The danger our society faces arises from more than "Islamo-fascists" or "homicide bombers" or whatever the American government has decided to call them this week, but also from our very own home-grown fanatics, some of whom—God help us—hold high elective office. We're in a war in Iraq right now because our president (whose "favorite philosopher," he says, is Jesus Christ) consulted his "Higher Father" and apparently believes he got the go-ahead from God Himself. Article I of our Constitution's Bill of Rights is under *daily* assault; there are people in all three branches of the American government who actually believe—and proclaim—that the separation of church and state is nothing more than a secular humanist conspiracy.

Who can we call upon to stand up for our essential freedoms—to protect our Constitution, as our president falsely swore to do, against all enemies, foreign and domestic? How can anyone possibly forge a political movement—an army of tolerance and intellectual freedom—out of the bewildering variety of atheists, agnostics, Wiccans and Druids, Asatru, Zoroastrians, liberal Christians, Zen Buddhists, and the gods alone might guess how many others who have good reason to fear the rise of fundamentalism? How can we stand against the relentless assault from all flavors of fanatic?

The answer is, of course, that *we* can't—but you can. In this fight the good guys don't *need* an army. All we need is you.

War is the crucible of character, and you are the Master Chief.

After decades of intensive textual analysis, literary historians have finally reached a consensus that *Heroes Die, Blade of Tyshalle, Caine Black Knife*, the Barra & Co. novels, *Star Wars: The New Jedi Order: Traitor, Star Wars: Shatterpoint*, and *Star Wars: Revenge of the Sith* were in fact not written by **Matthew Woodring Stover** at all, but by another man of the same name.

Kieron Gillen

PLANETARY OBJECTS IN THE REAR VIEW MIRROR

Our Distorted Preconceptions of Halo

Long before Halo *became a phenomenon, many were skeptical that a game developed by Microsoft could be all that good. This is the story of how the opinion leaders came around.*

LOS ANGELES. IT'S E3, 2003. Several thousand games journalists and similar industry professionals are crammed like particularly pallid sardines into Microsoft's press conference. The next few years of their plans are being explained on the big screen. Presentations are interrupted by sporadic whoops, because they always are. American games journalists whoop. The English element, of which I'm a part, sits back wearing a mask of cynical professionalism as a disguise for hangovers. *Halo 2* footage plays, and the whooping increases in pace. And, halfway into the demo, *it* happens.

Master Chief picks up a second weapon and starts blowing Covenant away with it.

Dual Wield! DUAL FUCKING WIELD!

The place goes crazy. The gentleman to my left grabs the railing in front of him and gasps, "Oh MY God." I look around, feeling like a mild-mannered vicar who's somehow found himself at an Aztec blood sacrifice. Dignity has left the building, the crowd doing everything short of throwing handfuls of ejaculate at the stage. My colleagues are just as bemused by this mass display of breast-beating. It's the sort of reaction that would be a tad extreme for the announcement of world peace.

If you asked me for my least favorite memory related to *Halo*, that would be it: abstract adults acting in such a manner, all because of such a basically meaningless improvement; the sort of improvement that looks great on the box but ultimately means nothing. *Halo*'s expansive charms had nothing to do with such simple crowd-pleasing, and to see people—my peers!—en masse seem to forget it, was just *embarrassing*. Didn't they get it? Or, alternatively, didn't *I* get it?

You see, it wasn't always like that. There was a time no one outside of Bungie cared about *Halo*. Or if they did, they cared for no reason at all. Or the wrong reason. Or jumped to some reason from the slightest of evidence. Or for a reason they made up inside the warped mush inside their heads. Or hated it, due to one of the same reasons.

Elsewhere in this book, I'd imagine someone will be talking about *Halo*'s prehistory as an SF RTS and similar. That's essential and concrete, but it's also what's been documented. That's history. But there's another history of *Halo*: a history of conceptions. More than any other cultural form, video games are hyped massively in advance of releases. Games will be part of the general conversation for *years* before anyone gets to play them. This is a history of *Halo* told through rumor and expectation—the forgotten parts of what we all said to each other in message boards and in pubs and defended to the death for no good reason. It's worth remembering that before it was the sort of modern classic that could provoke mass ecstasy by showing its lead character fire two guns at once, it was—at different times—the fresh-faced new contender, the sell-out, the castrated wreck of a game, and the subject of bribery conspiracies.

I'm a games journalist, if you'll pardon the phrase. I make most of my money from writing about video games. I've been doing it forever. I'm old enough to know better, but—alas—not smart enough. Back in 2000, I was working for the UK's *PC Gamer* as reviews editor. Sitting in an E3 hotel room with a margarita for company, I wrote the world's first cover feature on *Halo*. Now, if you put aside the small issue of it being a PC magazine, with *Halo*'s current standing, you'd think it was entirely natural to appear there. After all, which magazine wouldn't want the bragging rights of saying it did the world's first cover on one of the premiere games of its generation? But *Halo* only got a cover via a fluke.

Games magazines' covers are generally arranged far in advance. Game makers and editors barter editorial space for access. "We will give your magazine first access to review code, in exchange for the cover," says one half. "Okay, mate, you're on," says the other. It's a mutually equitable operation. It's also a mutually equitable operation that can go tits up with alarming regularity. And in the British press, covers really do matter. That sales are overwhelmingly via newsstands rather than subscriptions leads to a constant fight for audience on an issue-by-issue basis. What happens when you've promised the cover to three games? Well, the weeping art editor struggles to work out a way to create a collage of a race car, a marine, and some licensed, purple fruit into something that won't elicit disgusted vomiting in newsagents. It goes the other way just as often, when all the deals fall through and we're left with a blank space where a cover should be.

The space must be filled or else we die.

It was the E3 issue. The cover game—*Grand Prix 3*, which would proceed to drift back through the year, causing a series of scrambles to fill the space—had disappeared. *Halo* had been shown behind closed doors at E3. Clearly, from the first impressions, everyone knew it was going to be a perfect cover.

No, not really.

"My personal recollections—as I didn't see it—were of this very dull character in a game with a crap name. I was completely under advisement from the enthusiasm you and Matt had for it, and the newsgroups online," notes James Ashton, editor of *PC Gamer* at the time and now Future Group publisher, when asked about his decision, "and I think it was picked up on primarily on graphics rather than anything in the actual game."

"It's weird to think about it now, in that it's such a famous Xbox title, but before when we were looking at it...well, it wasn't even announced for that format yet," notes Ashton. "I remember before we went and saw it, and we were talking about it in the office, a lot of it was based around Bungie and their track record on the Mac. I remember looking at the company name for the first time and going, 'Hang on...what have they done?'" Bungie had a reputation. It was just a reputation that didn't really reach England. *Marathon* was as respected as a shooter could be on the Mac. Alas, for many PC games fans, that isn't actually very much. Their fantasy RTS myth in Europe was seen very much as a side-show to the main RTS events of Westood (*Command & Conquer* et al.) and Ensemble (*Age of Empires*).

Ashton's preconceptions were right in at least one way: what was primarily attracting people to *Halo* was a graphical kick. "I remember seeing the actual game demo at the time, and being completely blown away," remembers Matt Pierce, deputy editor of *PC Gamer* magazine at the time (now a publisher of *Future*). "I remember not believing that what we'd seen was actually real. And thinking—like pretty much everyone did with the Playstation stuff at last year's E3—that it was target footage rather than actual in game stuff." The demo was particularly spectacular. Forget the fact that I had six pages to fill from a twenty-minute interview with Bungie, where both tape-recorders died and we were reduced to scribbling notes in proto-shorthand; clearly, I was going to over-elaborate any fact I had to just to hit the word count. I was a little bit taken with *Halo*'s graphics. To my embarrassment, it's the text-based version of the crowd's excitement that *Halo 2*'s dual-wield provoked.

You want to hear some quotes, don't you?

Bollocks:

"Every second of the game, I've seen drips with silicon sex, sleek like a vinyl Concorde," I rant. "It's an orchestrated phallic über-assault, thrusting through your optic nerve to burst every one of your neurons with sheer pleasure. It's a luscious cruise missile launched from Bungie's headquarters, jetting across the Atlantic, into your flat, down your esophagus to explode your heart into a million fragments of love. In motion, *Halo* makes everything you've ever gazed upon lovingly in tawdry. It raises the bar of excellence through the ceiling, leaving its fellow competitors straining their necks at the heavens. After seeing *Halo*, the world looks ugly."

There's another paragraph of it, too. I was young. Also, as mentioned earlier, drinking a margarita. Also—my only real defense—I believed it. At E3 2000, *Halo* was so ahead of anything we'd seen, hyperbole was the only way to be honest. "It's weird," notes Matt Pierce, "we see things so far ahead of its time at E3, and we're blown away. We think...Christ, if only you could release it *now*."

Beneath that, there were elements that were somewhat questionable. Take the at-the-time-unnamed Master-Chief character. "I couldn't get over the fact you were playing a character whose face you couldn't see," remembers Matt. "It was against the then-current trend of character in game. He was less characterized even than the Doom Marine, who at least had a face and some kind of identity."

There was another trend that *Halo* ended up being, if not against, at least not interested in. It was also something in which people, in the excitement of the time, believed it *was* interested. If you want the primary misconception between what people believed *Halo* was, and what it actually ended up being, you look at the belief that it would somehow be an enormous sprawling 3D world. The Arc of the Halo in the distance? That'd actually be part of the game. "I actually thought you'd be able to walk forever around the world," recalls Matt. "This ringworld in the background would cycle around and it'll be like that scene in 2001, where he's walking upside down on the big revolving thing. That you'll be able to walk *forever* in one direction, then be back where you started. Only it wasn't a big freeform world. It had levels. I think we were all caught up with the next generation of games." It's something that people simply presumed it would do. "It's like *Outcast* [Infograme's *Zelda*-for-adults SF game]. Huge open-plan worlds were the new thing," recalls Ashton. "The whole concept that the larger the world, the more interesting things would be. That was the idea *du jour*."

Even now, you occasionally hear a PC games purist argue that this is what it would have been if it stayed on the one true format. Looking through the feature when it was still on the PC, there's simply no hint of it. Bungie goes deliberately out of its way to refute it, with the only living-world aspects referenced being bits of alien fauna.

The moment it went live, the article was almost certainly the single longest thing that had been written about *Halo* outside of its own design docs. Its cover was striking, with great art—always a bugbear for games' magazines—provided by Bungie. Coverline: "Meet the game of the year."

Three weeks after the magazine hits the street, Microsoft announced that it had purchased Bungie and *Halo* would be an Xbox exclusive.

I'd say that heavy drinking ensued, if we, the magazine, didn't already have a drinking culture that was challenging our livers on a daily basis.

The *Halo* issue ended up being the lowest-selling issue of the year; it probably would have been anyway. "New intellectual property on the cover of mainstream games magazines—as *PC Gamer* was at the time— isn't a good idea," argues Ashton. Video games are the cultural form where sequels often outperform their original incarnations. The same is true in terms of selling magazines: if the game on the cover has a "2" after it, sales are normally higher. Not that it didn't serve a purpose. "We went through a good period of breaking stuff, which in retrospect was brilliant, but didn't sell as well as we wanted," laments Matt. "It's strange to look back at *Halo* and say we did that first. Same as *Half-life*. We were the first mag to do a cover on that, years before everyone else did one." It's worth noting that the *Half-life* issue didn't sell, either.

But *Halo* was off to the Xbox. *PC Gamer* turned its attention elsewhere, and it was at this point I pretty much forgot *Halo* for a couple of years. Damn the treacherous bitch that dared leave us so.

Now an Xbox game, *Halo* had a different set of preconceptions with which to deal. People from a PC-game background could be excited by *Halo*. But from a more pure-console background, it was easy to be dismissive about it—and Microsoft's entrance into the world of video games, generally. Ste Curran, now creative director at Kuju Games, had recently joined the high-end, esteemed, multi-format British magazine *Edge* as a writer. While stronger than most writers, his reaction was commonplace in those who prefer a joypad to keyboard-and-mouse at the time.

"I first remember seeing a trailer when it was still on PC and being quite disinterested," Curran recalls. "I remember looking and thinking *Oh—another PC FPS. That's not my sort of thing.* I was quite detached from the whole thing, as I knew I'd never review it or have anything to do with it, as big, macho cyborg games aren't my forte." When, weeks later it moved to the Xbox, he was similarly unmoved. "I don't remember having any feelings at all," he says. "People's feelings towards the Xbox were that it was a PC in the box...so a PC FPS played with a joypad wasn't something which filled me with a great deal of excitement."

At this point, *Halo* virtually disappeared off the radar. "It had an enormous hype in the early days, but one of the advantages it did have was when it was picked up by Microsoft...it then had a year of anonymity," notes Ashton, who was copying *Halo*'s defection, moving from *PC Gamer* to launching the *Official Xbox Magazine*. "The game disappeared off the radar and was able to develop in peace, which doesn't normally happen for many other highly anticipated games...."

Its next real public appearance was at E3 2003. Last year's beautiful boy returned with something to live up to. An initial glance at the reports from the show doesn't really reveal how disastrous a showing it was, except through understanding of the secret code of video game previews. For example, Gamespot's hands-on experience is uniformly positive, apart from a passing comment that "the framerate took a hit during large explosions, but it was pretty minor and will hopefully be cleaned up by the time the game is released." The Golden Rule of previews in most of the mainstream press: if there's anything even slightly critical, it's something that, if it isn't fixed, will probably kill the game. There's an element of attempted fairness to this. By definition, it's a look at a game that's not finished. How fair is it to prejudge the game seriously? There's an element of self-interest to it, too. A writer may lose a degree of access if he spouts the opinions he would in the pub in the magazine, as the company reels from an unexpected media onslaught.

What were many people really thinking at E3? Well, take these quotes from the more left-field Gamecritic's Ben Hopper's coverage of *Halo*:

> By far the biggest joke of the show for me was Bungie's long-awaited Xbox title, *Halo*.
>
> Not only did *Halo*'s frame rate grind to a halt when the action got heavy, but [John] Howard had the gall to point out how amazing the lens flare looked when you stare at the game's sun. Wow, lens flare—we haven't seen that before in games have we?
>
> Playing the game only reinforced my negative reaction to this really ordinary experience. Not only is the control scheme awkward, but the split-screen mode looks like a Nintendo 64 game. The frame rate routinely froze during the action, and it sputtered along the rest of the time.

Ouch.

This proved to be the most memorable period for James Ashton, when it turned up at E3 "in a form that was so broken that it almost killed it." Ashton laments, "It was running between 13–15 FPS in multiplayer. Microsoft had taken the decision to devote a significant amount of floor space solely on the multiplayer, and people were going up to it, playing it for a bit, and just walking away. It was borderline unplayable it was running so slowly."

The final months only slowly exposed *Halo*. Even for the official magazines working on pre-launch mags, it was difficult to get access to anything approaching code. And when it finally turned up on Ashton's *Official Xbox Magazine*'s desk, what was shown was more than a little limited. "It was just that one level," recalls Ashton. "It played brilliantly—as well as it did in the final game—but it was just one level. Our suspicions were beginning to be aroused. This level is really good...once you got used to the control system. Again, that's something that put a lot of the console gamers off at the previous year at E3. Not many people were used to playing FPSs with dual analogue sticks."

You see, the trouble at E3 wasn't just the technical problems of multiplayer. It's easy to forget that *Halo*, in terms of pure mechanisms, was the first FPS that operated even vaguely like a traditional PC control system. "It was the first console FPS which really had mastered an approximation of the control you get with the keyboard and mouse," notes Ashton. "*Goldeneye* had been a good shot at it with one stick."

"*Alien Resurrection* on the PS1 might have been decent, as the way it was so difficult fitted neatly that you were meant to be terrified all the time, so when you were attacked you couldn't move around," Ste Curran said of precursors in terms of using dual analog control in this way. "You certainly can't remember the button combination to spin around. It wasn't just that *Halo* implemented much better than everyone else— they did—but because the Xbox's analogue sticks were well suited. And the game was designed for a slightly slower pace where you don't have to turn around." But no matter how well-suited it was, it was still too much to take in on the floors of E3.

When the final code arrived, barely before release, Ashton's doubts evaporated. "It was clear from then on in we had something absolutely huge on our hands," he recalls. "I can probably name three or four games which have ever arrived which have come to dominate the office environment and are played all the time. We played link-up *Halo* on four Xboxes more or less every lunch time and every evening for over a year." But official magazines aren't really where expectations are changed. An official magazine raving is one thing; no matter how good its intentions are, there's a level of cynicism whenever it applies the stratospheric marks. If there was an official Paramount film review magazine, it's unlikely you'd take its word as gospel.

Edge magazine is somewhat different. For an American reader, it's difficult to explain the standing *Edge* maintained in its thirteen years of publication. The nearest comparison is the defunct *Next Generation* magazine, which was an attempt to bring its format to the colonies. As good as *Next Generation* could be, it was never as deliberately postured or determinedly upmarket as *Edge*, whose ethos was perhaps best expressed by its original advertisements in the early nineties: "You may not like *Edge*. *Edge* isn't for everyone." In the end, *Edge* is the games magazine for people too embarrassed to buy most games magazines, both in terms of aesthetics and content. And if you think that's a somewhat elitist stance, have a flick through a few magazines next time you're in a newsagent.

Most relevantly, *Edge* has arguably the strictest marking scheme in video game magazine history. Before the fall of 2001, only three games had ever scored full marks: *Mario 64*, *Zelda: Ocarina of Time*, and *Gran Turismo*. In the UK, *Edge* was as hard a core badge of quality as existed.

Halo was the fourth.

Behind the standard byline-less *Edge* review was Curran, who was just as amazed that he'd provided full marks as everyone else. It wasn't even a game he thought he'd ever play. "Why I ended up playing the game was that time of the year—because of Xbox launch and so much good stuff coming out on PS2—we ended up being overwhelmed," Curran says. "All our best freelancers were used. We didn't want to take it out of house anyway, and all the in-house reviewers either didn't want to play it or were busy with other games. By the time the console came in, it didn't fit with people's schedules. The only way I could get the game reviewed properly was to do it myself." Cue Curran paranoidly dragging the enormous machine, worried about being mugged by one of genteel Bath's half-dozen-tops career criminals.

He played it in an enormous session, lasting from ten in the morning to four in the afternoon before turning to his computer and sending an e-mail to the rest of the team. It was titled, "A list of things I consider wrong with *Halo*." The body copy was blank.

"I was worried because before that I'd always worried what it would feel like to review a ten out of ten game for *Edge*," Curran recalls. "We were really precious about those review scores. I couldn't imagine a time when I'd be approaching the team and saying, 'Guys...I think this is a ten out of ten.' It was when I sent that e-mail I wondered, *Curran, Oh shit. What am I going to do*?"

What he did was play the game more, working through all the game modes, before turning to multiplayer and link-up. "When I suggested it may be a ten out of ten, everyone was aghast; then one by one they all played it themselves," Curran notes. "Joao [Diniz-Sanches, *Edge* editor] spent a long time on it and...well, decided I may be right."

The mark went out, and immediate accusations of foul play were claimed by the *Edge* fanbase. This was simply unimaginable: that Microsoft—*Microsoft*—could arrive on the scene with a game fit to sit at the same table as Mario creator Miyamoto's best. Clearly, someone had to have paid someone else off. "Part of the reason people were so annoyed was that people couldn't imagine it as...well, a first-person shooter [game] had never got a ten out of ten," Curran notes. "*Goldeneye* and *Half-life* had both got nines. Suddenly, a console FPS from Microsoft, the great enemy, who'd had the temerity to infringe in this console space...this was the first? In a way, they were incredibly precious, too. *They* didn't want the ten out of ten to be polluted by Microsoft."

It was more difficult because *Edge*'s review sat alone. No one else had played it. "We reviewed it so far in advance of everyone else, we didn't have anyone else to back us up," Curran notes. "When the score came out, it was like a bolt from the blue." Its approach aggravated problems, too. When the review avoided specifics like the appearance of the Flood and the Sentinels, to avoid spoiling their introductions changes the game, it left some *Edge* readers scratching their heads. While explaining in general terms, it didn't give specific evidence that was required to convince. Of course, to actually have done that would have damaged the experience of playing the game. "I alluded to it and think it was the right decision to make," Curran argues.

Edge's review describes *Halo* as "the most important launch game for any console, ever." In its way, the *Edge* review was the most important *review* of a launch game for any console, ever. It gave Microsoft the one thing they couldn't actually buy: credibility.

"They were absolutely over the moon," Curran recalls. "I remember meeting Richard Teversham [of Microsoft Marketing] at the Xbox launch party. Teversham just put his arm around me and said, "I owe you my life." I don't believe Teversham does owe me his life, but I did wonder at the time whether I could trade that for an Xbox." There were none available for reviewers, causing *Edge* to go out and buy them en masse for £300 a pop. "Only to be caught like saps when the price dropped £100," Curran sighs, "but it was worth it. For six months of *Halo*, it was worth it. Effortlessly in my top-five games of all time."

It's at this point I rejoin the story, picking up my Xbox on the UK launch day almost solely on the basis of Curran's printed words. Everyone does. By then, with the UK release only in March, the game of whispers was already coming to an end throughout the world. As people picked up the joypad, one-by-one rumor and hearsay were transformed into actual experience. At which point it became the subject of the other essays of this book—a game to be played intensely by yourself, with friends, and eventually online; the modern classic. But once, it was only an idea, a dream, and, well, as anyone who twitched all night in the torment of a fever dream knows, there are some dreams that can be incredibly twisted.

Remember, this happens with *every* game. Few have had to journey across such tumultuous critical topography as *Halo*—from future messiah to pariah and back again in a couple of years, but all games flicker and warp in our communal imaginations. I don't expect these few collected reminisces to stop anyone from stating his or her belief that game-X is going to suck because of reason-Y loudly and persistently for the years up to the game's release, but hopefully, perhaps, quote a little self-awareness. You could be wrong; there is nothing wrong with being wrong. In fact, when a game as challenging and inspiring as *Halo* is what happens when you're wrong, we should be grateful.

After leaving *PC Gamer* magazine after reaching deputy editor, **Kieron Gillen** has since been working as a freelance journalist for organs as varied as *Eurogamer* and the *Escapist*, *Wired*, and the *Guardian*. He makes a living, of sorts.

Paul Kix

HAVE GUN, WILL TRAVEL

Want to make a good living playing Halo? *Matt Leto does.*

ZYOS PLAYS THE VIDEO GAME *HALO*, plays it better than anyone in the world. His mother, Rhonda, watched him dominate the military combat game in San Francisco last year at the World Cyber Games—the gaming Olympics—and because of her status, because she is the mother of Zyos, Rhonda became a *de facto* celebrity herself. She didn't expect that. She doesn't understand the game, in which you kill enemy combatants on your own or on a team. Yet gamers from across the world approached her. Zyos is a great champion, they said. One of them, an earnest kid from New Zealand, sought her out to tell her he'd flown to San Francisco to study Zyos's playing tendencies.

Zyos's father, Steve, once got a call at work from a man in Oklahoma. The man in Oklahoma wanted Zyos to play his fourteen-year-old son. The man told Steve he would pay Zyos, pay him anything he wanted, if he would play one game of *Halo*—just one—against his son. Zyos, after all, was the kid's hero.

Zyos, while vacationing in Italy over Thanksgiving, went a week without playing *Halo 2* on Xbox Live. Microsoft makes Xbox, and Xbox Live is the company's latest and best advance. It allows a gamer to plug his Xbox into an Internet cable and play, say, *Halo 2*, against anyone in the world. It also keeps track of how often a gamer plays, and makes that information available to all others.

Over Thanksgiving, on Day Five without Zyos, the message boards of the online world were abuzz with rumors. Zyos has quit. Zyos is playing under a different name. Zyos is dead. Five pages of this, growing more fevered as it went, until one of Zyos's handlers, one of the people in the business of "building Zyos's brand," logged on.

"Guys," he said. "Zyos is fine. He's just on vacation."

It sounds like apocrypha, doesn't it? But it's not. Zyos is as talented, as sought after, as any myth you could make about him. And in the coming years, you will hear about Zyos. For one, he lives in Allen, Texas, and he's practicing even tonight. Look at him. He's hunched over in his chair again, shouting.

"Bombs down in front of our base! There's a sniper on the ridge. . . . Sniper's dead. . . . He's coming after your flag! There's a ghost who just went in. . . . Ghost is dead."

He has the headset on, the one with the microphone that wraps around the ear and drops down to his mouth, and on the television screen is *Halo 2*, the shoot-'em-up head-to-head sequel to *Halo* that racked up sales of $125 million in its first day on the market, and in the air there's a slightly stale stench, the sort that comes from a twenty-one-year-old who plays the game for hours behind a closed bedroom door.

But on the walls are his first-place plaques and oversize checks for $20,000. And in an hour he'll leave his parents' house, where he still lives, drive to Dallas, and sign a contract with a company called Check Six, which will pay his airfare and hotel fees in 2005 whenever he plays *Halo* for money.

Zyos plays *Halo* for a living, but the checks he earns are signed under his given name, Matt Leto. Major League Gaming signed Leto to play *Halo* professionally in the fall of 2003, when Leto was nineteen. MLG is a professional gaming league that holds tournaments across the nation and last year handed out $175,000 in total purses in its inaugural season—a season that concluded with MTV broadcasting its championship, further convincing MLG personnel that theirs is the new X Games. Hell, the new NASCAR.

MLG loves Leto. In fact, the league was so confident he would succeed as a professional, it signed him before it held its first event. Now, one year later, a year in which Leto dominated all comers in single and team play, a year in which he won MLG's single-player *Halo* championship and retained his title as Best *Halo* Player Alive at the World Cyber Games, MLG has built a marketing campaign around Leto, staked its future on him. "He's the face of our league," says Mike Sepso, the CEO and co-founder of Major League Gaming.

It's not a bad move, for a few reasons. For one, Leto's competitive as hell. Even the best *Halo* players in the world say Leto's drive far exceeds their own. He has no girlfriend. *Halo* is his focus. Even tonight, one hour before he meets Check Six executives, even as he practices Halo with his teammates spaced across the country—all of them connected to one another by plugging in their game systems, their Xboxes, to an Internet cable—even on this self-described "fun" night of game play, Leto's elbows are on his knees; he's shouting at his teammates; he has no time for idle chitchat with the visitor who's stopped by. There are still competitors to best.

Second, and perhaps surprising, Leto's not a nerd. He's an athlete. He lettered in swimming at Allen High and still holds the build: his shoulders stretch wide the white T-shirt he wears tonight, and his quads and calves fill out his sweat pants. He's handsome enough, about five-foot-eight, with the olive complexion of an Italian heritage. He sweeps his dark hair straight back, and a day's growth of stubble is forever on his chin. He's personable, too—once you yank the controller away. "He's very laid-back," says Kim Murphy, an associate producer at Worldsport HD, a satellite channel that followed Leto around for a documentary it will air next month.

Last, Leto has a wisdom beyond his years. At seventeen he told his parents he would one day make a living playing *Halo*, though MLG did not exist at the time and there was no reason to believe it ever would. But Leto's wisdom most often presents itself in his speech. For someone who's played video games since he was four, sometimes for twelve hours a day, Leto is surprisingly articulate. "Oh, he's very well-spoken," Murphy says. It's incisive, his speech, in no way cluttered with the stammerings and non sequiturs of his peers, gaming or otherwise. He has a deep and confident voice, too. But it always sounds flat, as if he's heard before how lucky he is and is tired of hearing it again. It's for these reasons—the directness of speech, the tone of voice—that people often find Matt Leto cold upon meeting him.

"Yeah, we're working on that," Sepso says.

He's not kidding. MLG has hired a public relations firm from Los Angeles to train Leto in speaking to the media. Sepso and his staff talk openly about creating a marketable image for their star—an image similar to that of skateboarder Tony Hawk: pioneer, best ever, industry spokesman.

It sounds crazy to talk this way about a kid playing a video game. But it was crazy twenty years ago to talk about a skateboarder like this. Besides, have you seen the stats? They're crazy, too. According to the National Institute on Media and the Family, 92 percent of boys play video games. There are 108 million people over the age of thirteen in the United States playing today, and 13 million of those are "hard-core," people who spend upward of fifteen hours a week under the glow of a television or computer screen.

And the craziest thing of all? The money that's out there. Last year, Matt Leto, college dropout, cleared more than $80,000 playing *Halo*, the earnings a combination of tournament winnings and endorsement deals. That spoke to him. Talk all you want about his competitive drive, the notoriety; it's the promise of money, and more money, that finds him in that stale bedroom night after night. If all goes as planned, he figures, he should make well more than $100,000 this year. Just for playing a video game.

"After all, the hackneyed first story inevitably is about the novelty of video gamers playing for cash, but what is the second story about this phenomenon going to be about?"
—*Electronic Gaming Business*, October 22, 2003

Well, more stories, certainly, will be written about Matt Leto, so maybe the next one, for a change of pace, could focus on his driving to Houston, or Detroit, or flying to Seattle, on his dime, just to practice *Halo* against opponents living in those cities. Leto, of course, doesn't have to fly anywhere. With an Xbox plugged into the Internet, he can play anyone, in any city, at any time. But the truth is, when he does that, within seconds there are twenty people who see he's online. And all twenty will want to play against him. And none will be any good. It's a big waste of his time when he's preparing for a tournament. No, far better for Zyos to seek out the best players in the States and go to them.

Still, that's not telling the whole story, if we're worried about moving beyond the hackneyed first attempt of profiling Matt Leto. Because Zyos does plug his Xbox into the Internet to practice. He plugs it in and "closes the room," meaning only the select few he deems worthy can practice against him. So why fly to Seattle? To videotape the practice matches, of course.

Yeah, maybe the second story will be about Matt Leto flying to Seattle before the World Cyber Games 2004, practicing for a week against Stephen Booth, a world-renowned player (and a freshman at the University of Washington), and videotaping every match. The two played for twelve hours a day during Zyos's visit. But what Booth remembers about Leto's stay is his analyzing the matches, reviewing the tape that had recorded every move, every shot, and looking for weaknesses in his game and Booth's.

"He puts in more time than anyone," Booth says. Before Leto's visit, he had never thought to record his preparatory games. Yet in Zyos's closet there are more than twenty tapes of practice matches.

"He does all the things that all the other kids won't do. And that's why he wins," Steve Leto says.

The second story will probably mention Leto's youth, how, at four, Matt got a Nintendo with the famous *Super Mario Brothers* included. He'd play and play and play the game. Then conquer it and ask for another. Then conquer the second game and ask for a third. Then conquer that and ask for a fourth. Soon, games like *Zelda*, games that take months to beat, Leto would be done with overnight. Yet he'd need more challenges, more games. "What's the point," his parents asked, "if you're going to conquer it tomorrow?" But in the end, they always gave in.

In an effort to show a balanced childhood, perhaps the second story will talk about the real-life games he played. Every team sport you can name. But, truth be told, "He's never been much of a team player," his mother says. Too many kids goofing around. Too many kids screwing up in key situations, times when Leto would have done better if only he had the ball.

But in individual sports, he controlled everything. Individual sports, he loved. That's why he swam at Allen High, even though Allen didn't have a pool and practice was held in McKinney at 5:15 every morning, which meant Leto had to be out the door at 4:45, a gruesome hour by any account but made worse by his closing Chuck E. Cheese's every night at 10:30.

"He never missed a practice," Rhonda Leto says. Her son was a three-year letter winner in three events.

School bored him. Yet Karen Bradley, house principal at Allen High, says he was "one of the smartest kids I've ever come across." And Brent Mitchell, Leto's swim coach, remembers Matt more as an intellectual than a swimmer. He memorized the book on school policy, Mitchell says, not because he had to but because he wanted to. "He made a game of it," Mitchell says, every morning explaining to the swim coach what he could and couldn't get away with, testing Mitchell to see if he knew the rules as well as he should. If Mitchell doubted him, Leto would say, "Look in the book."

"Verbatim," Mitchell says. "To the tooth and nail of it exactly. It always drove me crazy."

It would be pretty amazing, too, if the next story could contrast Leto's love for knowing the rules in the real world with his love of breaking them in gaming. Leto knew his games so well, he knew where to find glitches in the programmer's code. That's when he got really good at gaming, because every game has glitches. When he properly exploited them, Leto's finishing scores were among the best in the world.

At seventeen, Leto broke the world record for points in a game called *Crazy Taxi*. Elated, he snapped a photo of his score and mailed it to Twin Galaxies, the official scorekeeper of all video games and publisher, every few years, of a book on gaming world records. But Twin Galaxies said Leto's photo wasn't good enough. It needed video proof. So Leto plugged the VCR into his Sega Dreamcast and broke the record he'd taken a picture of. Then, because he "always wanted to be the best at something," Leto says, he spent a year breaking as many scores as he could.

"He probably holds over 800 world records," says Walter Day, the chief scorekeeper and founder of Twin Galaxies. Day doesn't have a definitive count because, three years later, Twin Galaxies is still combing through Leto's tapes, more than thirty of them. "Matt Leto may be the premier video game player in the world," he says.

Most guys hold world records in racing games or shooting games; never, Day says, in both racing and shooting games. Leto holds records across the video game spectrum. Any sort of game—ones based on the most kills, the best time, the highest points—on any sort of console: GameCube, Xbox, PlayStation, the old Nintendo Entertainment System. Leto has world records for them all, some for an entire game, some for an individual level. "No matter the game, he will be among the top 2 percent at it in a matter of days," says Robert Mruczek, the chief referee of Twin Galaxies.

And the glitches he knows. Maybe the second story will mention them; hell, it could be about nothing else. Here, one example will suffice: In *Crazy Taxi 2*, Leto found a glitch, or, as he says, an "exploit" that's invisible—traditionally, these are very difficult to find, Mruczek says—and it's in the sky above the road.

"Less than five people in the world know where this is," Mruczek says.

Yet he's humble about this and all those records, and maybe the next story on Matt Leto, if it needs a telling anecdote, will highlight how he never told his parents of the many exploits he knew or the records he held.

"Really?" Rhonda Leto says. "Oh, my gosh. I had no clue. I had no clue."

Never told Major League Gaming, either.

"No," says Erik Semmelhack, MLG's senior vice president, after a pause. "I didn't know that."

At first, there were two of them, Mike Sepso and Sundance DiGiovanni, playing *Halo* in the summer of 2002 in DiGiovanni's downtown New York loft, the one with the projection screen that made the play larger than life and all the more addictive. Betting on their matches, where each was a soldier trying to kill the other, led to friends stopping by to place their own bets on who would win. Which led to more friends stopping by to gamble. Which led to still more friends, some of whom just wanted to watch. *When are you two doing this again?* the friends would ask at the end of the night. *This is fun.* Which led to an epiphany.

When will we watch the best in the world on a projection screen?

Sepso had been the co-CEO of Gotham Broadband, a nationwide broadband service, and DiGiovanni was the company's creative director. But they left Gotham to answer that question. Over the next year, they flew across the country, hitting up every local video game tournament they could find. They took notes, talked about the passion the gamers had, how they played for the competition of it, because the cash prizes handed out—when they were handed out—were often less than advertised. They talked about a professional gaming league, a league that would organize tournaments across the nation, where each tournament was open to any competitor, provided the competitor paid an entrance fee. They talked about a league that would draw sponsors to hand out cash prizes unseen in any local tournament, a league that would take the best players from each game and help the players find endorsements in exchange for wearing league memorabilia. They talked about a league, like NASCAR, that would highlight the personalities of its players over the intricacies of its game.

On August 3, 2003, Sepso and DiGiovanni took a limo to a *Halo* tournament in Saddle Brook, New Jersey. Zyos was there. He'd finished seventh in the individual tournament, and his team, The Dream Team, the team no one could beat, the team that made a video of itself playing and watched as the tape was downloaded more than 80,000 times on the Web—this team was once more in the championship game.

But it lost that day to Shoot to Kill, a team formed for the express purpose of defeating The Dream Team. Undeterred, Sepso and DiGiovanni ushered the four teenagers—two from Texas, two from Kansas—into the limo and took them to a steak house in Times Square, where the pitch was made: we've formed a professional gaming league, and we want you four as our first signed players.

And so a new industry began.

Which is not to say professional gaming leagues didn't already exist. South Korea has three. It has a governing body for the leagues, the Korean e-Sports Association, which ranks the standings for the 218 professional gamers in the country. Here in the States, there's the Cyberathlete Professional League, a league started in 1997 by a thirty-seven-year-old Dallasite named Angel Munoz. But there's a major difference between Munoz's league and MLG: the system through which games are played.

CPL is a personal computer-based league, meaning its athletes—and Munoz argues they *are* athletes—play their games on computers. MLG is a console-based league, meaning its athletes—MLG makes the same argument—play their games on a console system, such as a PlayStation or Xbox. Both are successful: MLG will hold tournaments for three game titles this year, for a total purse of $250,000; CPL has a $1.2 million ten-city worldwide tour in 2005 for its seven-game roster. But the leagues attract different sorts of gamers. Simply put, PC players tend on average to be more—how to put this?—computer-literate than their console counterparts.

Their sponsors reflect that. CPL is endorsed by CompUSA, Hitachi, and Intel. Last year, MLG had Converse as a title sponsor.

"Each is a different culture," says Daiquiri Jackson, promotions manager for GameStop, a video game retailer that's endorsed both leagues.

Yet both leagues are not without their critics. Doug Gentile is the director of research at the National Institute on Media and the Family. "We have an obesity epidemic in this country. That's not my word. That's the National Institutes of Health's," he says. "And one of the reasons is likely to be screen time.... And now we're giving kids more incentive to play more."

Mary Story, one of the nation's foremost obesity researchers at the University of Minnesota, agrees that the leagues could lead to more kids sitting around but argues ours is a sedentary culture regardless of age or interest. To single out MLG over, say, corporate America, which asks its employees to sit in a cubicle for eight hours a day, is hypocritical, she says.

Gentile won't let MLG or any other league off that easily. He points to the work of Dr. Paul Lynch at the University of Oklahoma. Lynch has studied the physiological effects of video games on teenagers for fifteen years. In 1999, he published a study suggesting violent video games might cause heart problems later in life.

Violent games, like *Halo*, raise one's adrenaline level. And adrenaline, the study says, is nothing more than fatty acids that are used as an energy source. Yet these fatty acids released into the bloodstream are not acted upon by the gamer's muscles, because the gamer is sitting and playing, not running or jumping or fighting. Since no muscle will use them, the fatty acids in the end make their way through the liver, where they are converted to cholesterol. "This could be a precursor for heart disease," Gentile writes via e-mail.

Could be, but the scientific community needs to further parse the data. In the interim, MLG is willing to respond to a more general question: Is paying people to play video games bad for the health of the nation?

"My initial knee-jerk reaction is 'Give me a break,'" says DiGiovanni, two years after his epiphany the executive vice president of MLG. "We're encouraging kids to do what they already love. And a small amount of those kids can make a living at it." MLG has signed seventeen people to be pro-gamers. Yet DiGiovanni says none of the seventeen signed, nor the thousands more who attend MLG events, is a pasty-white, obese basement dweller.

"These guys are competitive. These are guys who compete in other sports," he says. And then, almost with an air of resignation, "Just come to one of our events."

Zyos has the rocket launcher. Mathieu Hebbada, from France, runs the halls of this abandoned, darkened warehouse with a shotgun. The game is tied at fourteen, and if Zyos scores one more kill, he's crowned World Cyber Games *Halo* Champion 2003 and awarded $20,000. Zyos settles under a ramp, points his weapon toward a second-floor window, and waits.

Tournament *Halo* is played in one of two ways. What Zyos is playing now is single-player *Halo*. Before him is a television screen of his position in the warehouse, and in the screen's bottom right corner, Mathieu Hebbada's position. In single-player, the first gamer to score fifteen kills wins. Then there's multiplayer *Halo*. The difference between multiplayer and single-player is you're on a team in multiplayer. A two-man team or a four-man team. Together, you seek and kill the other team. The first one to score fifty kills wins. Zyos, in a couple of weeks, will play for The Dream Team in a tournament in New York, but it's this sort of tournament in Seoul, the single-player one, where he excels.

The weapons one uses—pistol, shotgun, rocket launcher, what have you—are the same for both single- and multiplayer tournaments and are found throughout a level's landscape. Zyos discovered that certain weapons are made available at certain parts of levels at certain times. But the times when they're available never change. In other words, it's clockwork. Zyos put a clock above his television one day, ran to the right spots, waited for the weapons to materialize and collected them all before his opponent could get any. Easy game. Today, in 2003, it's the most common exploit known to *Halo* players.

Still, despite his genius, Zyos's parents remain skeptical. They doubt their son will ever make a living playing video games. They doubt the promises of MLG. Yet here he is in a packed auditorium in Seoul, South Korea, with thousands more watching him over the Internet, with a chance at $20,000. For Zyos, it's a start.

He focuses the rocket launcher's scope onto the right half of the window. Seconds pass. Hebbada hasn't studied the different levels as thoroughly as Zyos, doesn't know that by walking in front of this window, he's inadvertently walking into the line of. . . .

A blast from Zyos's gun. And the game is over. The thousands in attendance, watching the action on a projection screen, cheer.

One year and two months later, sitting in his parents' living room in Allen, Matt Leto says, "That [win] changed everything." Changed his parents' perception of his dream, changed the way in which he practiced—if anything else, he became more obsessive, more thorough after World Cyber Games 2003. He gave himself to *Halo*.

The year that followed Seoul was a blur of frequent-flyer miles and first-place checks. By the time San Francisco hosted World Cyber Games 2004 in October, Leto had won roughly $10,000 in MLG tournaments, in both single and team play. He'd also formed and disbanded seven teams, because, despite their success, they still didn't live up to Leto's expectations. And he'd dropped out of Collin County Community College, because he could stand to win $40,000 more at WCG San Francisco and the MLG Championship in New York if he practiced nonstop.

It started in 2000, and 2004 marked the first year any city outside Korea hosted the World Cyber Games. Roughly 700 gamers from sixty countries qualified for the five-day, eight-game event. San Francisco held it in the Bill Graham Civic Auditorium, next to City Hall. There was $412,600 in total purses.

Leto's family came. Steve and Rhonda, younger sister Megan and brother Taylor. It was the first time any Leto would watch Matt in person. He'd breezed through the qualifying rounds in Miami and Long Beach, California. He was the favorite to win WCG again. Wherever he went in San Fran, a camera crew from Worldsport HD followed, shooting footage for a documentary on the Games.

Zyos beat his first opponent, Nelson Triana of Canada, 15–1. Then Yoonho Choi of South Korea, 15–3. Even if he lost his next match, against fellow American Stephen Booth, Zyos would advance. The first day of *Halo* at WCG is a round-robin of four players per bracket, and no one else was 2–0 with one match left.

Zyos lost his match to Booth 15–6. The loss had its upside, though. It meant both Americans would advance to the championship bracket. But the gamers watching, especially the Canadian Nelson Triana, now eliminated from the next round, thought something wasn't right. Why had Zyos, normally a conservative player, one who waited for his opponents to expose themselves, become the aggressor against Booth, accidentally running into his fire? And weren't the two, away from the controllers, friends? And to prepare for WCG, hadn't Leto flown to Seattle and spent a week practicing at Booth's house? Maybe they'd formed some sort of pact up there, to make sure they both advanced.

Andrew Mayeda covered WCG 2004 for the *Ottawa Citizen*. He quoted three gamers who thought Leto threw the game. He talked to one of the match's referees, "and I have to be careful how I phrase this," Mayeda says, "but I suspect he thought that Matt threw the game, too."

The referee in question is Cody Walker, also a Canadian. Leto says, "Look, both of the referees were Canadian. Nelson was Canadian. The map 'the individual level on which his match against Booth was played' is almost like a coin toss as to who wins it. Winning on that map is based more on luck than skill. It's completely false that I threw the match....I lose games. Just to say I'm unbeatable is wrong." No, there was no pact between him and Booth, he says. And Booth's practicing against him for a week—could it not mean that Booth had learned in that time how to beat Zyos?

In any case, in a decision they refused to explain, WCG officials ordered another round-robin among Zyos, Booth, and Triana.

Zyos and Triana advanced.

That night Triana drove to Best Buy and bought a television so he could practice on his own. He went to bed around 4 A.M. Zyos was up that late, too. But he wasn't practicing; he'd prepared enough for WCG. He was playing poker.

Didn't affect his gaming, though. He dominated his quarterfinal and semifinal opponents the next day; in the semifinal match, Sebastian Droschak, from Germany, failed to score a point.

Zyos faced Triana for the championship. Triana had beaten out Dave Walsh to get there, the American some viewed as better than Zyos. But Zyos had already beaten Triana, and he'd learned something while watching the Canadian's other games: Whenever his match was the match displayed on the movie-style projection screen, the one hanging down from the roof so the thousands in attendance could watch from a distance rather than huddle around the television on which their favorite gamer played, whenever his match was the featured one, Triana would get nervous, play tentatively, be afraid to make a mistake with God and all of the Bill Graham Civic Auditorium watching.

And if any match were to be on the projection screen, Zyos thought, it would be the championship one.

"Dad," he said before the match started, when Steve Leto worried his presence might screw up his son's concentration, "I've got this one."

Zyos was right. Triana was too nervous to eat before the match, and during it, as Andrew Mayeda of the *Citizen* wrote, "in a number of key confrontations, he couldn't finish Leto off despite having the advantage."

Zyos won 15–9 and 15–11, the fist pump he gave at the end the only real show of emotion from the whole tournament. Another $20,000 check was his. From October to October, factoring in the money he'd won from MLG, Matt Leto now made more playing video games than most people did in their first year out of college.

And he still had the MLG Championship in New York to consider.

He got to New York at four in the morning sick as all get-out. Leto spent the next few hours between the bed and the bathroom of his hotel suite. Then it was off to the MLG Championship, to which only the top-ranked players were invited.

The MTV and MLG people had wanted him to come earlier than the night before. MTV needed preliminary footage of Leto for the documentary on *Halo 2* it would later air, and it would really be great, really help the piece along, if Leto agreed to come a couple of days in advance. But Leto didn't agree. Said he needed to practice with his team, the Filthy Jackalopes, in Detroit. Said he wanted to be on top of his game. This from the guy who'd won WCG 2004 two weeks earlier.

So he stayed in Detroit. Stayed until he had to go, drove from Detroit to Manhattan thirteen hours across the country, carrying with him what would later be diagnosed as food poisoning.

The sickness "was coming out of everywhere," MLG's Erik Semmelhack says. In the morning, he took Leto to get a cup of coffee, then sat him down in the VIP section near the sound stage on West 12th Street where the tournament was about to begin.

He wore his winter jacket while he played. In the Free For All, the event where it's every man for himself, every man trying to score as many kills as possible while getting killed the fewest times possible, where two, four, or ten gamers can gang up on one to take him out, where it makes sense to do that—especially to Zyos, ranked first for the year in the Free For All Zyos nonetheless took the early lead. And never looked back.

To win the Free For All as Zyos won it, finishing some twenty kills better than the next gamer, "that's just, like, unheard of in any tournament setting," Adam Apicella, the vice president of operations for MLG, told MTV. "Let alone against seven of the best tournament players in the world. He just dominated the game, and I've never seen really a performance like that."

The win meant a bye into the Final Four of the single-player tournament. Dreary-eyed even when the MTV cameras were on him—he advanced to the championship match. And then won that 15–8.

"Yes!" he yelled, and pumped his fist a couple of times.

The weekend went well. An $8,000 check for his first-place finish in the single-player tournament. A $15,000 endorsement from Nokia for taking first. A $2,000 check for finishing the season ranked first overall. A $5,000 check to the Filthy Jackalopes for finishing second in the four-on-four tournament. (Fittingly, Zyos had a new team by December.)

And the money keeps coming. Semmelhack says Zyos is looking at "mid-five figures" in endorsements alone this year. And with MLG's tournament purse of $250,000 in 2005, Matt Leto, college dropout, professional *Halo* player, should be a six-figure twenty-two-year-old by year's end.

"I *am* lucky," he says. "But it takes a lot of skill, too."

Paul Kix was educated in the public schools of rural Iowa and is a 2003 graduate of Iowa State University. He interned at many places, most notably *ESPN the Magazine*, found permanent employment in Phoenix at *New Times*, and then, in 2004, moved to Dallas and the city's alt-weekly, the *Observer*. He is now associate editor at *D* magazine, Dallas's monthly magazine. In his office cube is a miniature Cadillac Escalade. It has spinners. Paul's proud of those spinners.

Kevin R. Grazier, Ph.D.

HALO SCIENCE 101

Kevin R. Grazier, scientist and science advisor to Battlestar Galactica,
explains how the science of Halo *works... and where it doesn't.*

SEVERAL YEARS AGO, after I'd performed a pair of planetarium shows
at Santa Monica College, several of the audience members and I retired
to a local restaurant to prolong our evening of astronomical fellowship.
The topic of conversation turned from the stars and planets to a round-
robin discussion of movies—in general, what kind of movies everyone
enjoyed and, specifically, what we had seen lately. By the sheer fact that
these people chose to spend their Friday evening attending planetarium
presentations to learn more about the universe, they obviously enjoyed
exercising their gray matter in their spare time. It was no surprise, then,
that the movies this crowd chose to see also tended towards the intellectual.

Because of our seating arrangement and the order of the topic's progression, I would be the last to speak. Since I was the only person at
the table with a Ph.D., there was an elevated air of expectation. What
would he say? Would he reveal a little-known documentary? Perhaps a
stimulating foreign film? Would he list one of the classics as his all-time
most cherished movie? In retrospect, the collective disappointment to

my less intellectual—and more "blue collar"—reply was astoundingly amusing. I simply said, "You know, I get enough intellectual stimulation at work, so when I go to the movies, I want to *see things explode.*"

Given my taste in movies, it isn't much of a stretch to imagine that I'm quite a fan of many of today's first-person-shooter video games. I'm a big fan of *Doom* and all its incarnations, for example. So, when *Halo: Combat Evolved* arrived on the scene—a video game that appeared on the surface to be a cross between *Ringworld* (one of the first science fiction books I ever read) and *Aliens* (my all-time favorite "shoot-'em-up" SF movie), I was all over it.

In fact, the case has been made—on several *Halo*-related Web sites, for example—that there isn't much about *Halo's* plotline that is original. There are elements of numerous science fiction books, movies, classical mythology, and even biblical references. *Halo* is an amalgam of all of these. In fact, we can find allusions to the *Alien* movies when the game is barely underway: the sergeant "motivating" the soldiers on the UNSC Cruiser, *Pillar of Autumn*, is remarkably similar to Sgt. Apone from *Aliens*, and if you look closely enough at the bulletin board behind the bridge on *Pillar of Autumn*, you can even make out a flyer for a missing cat named Jonesy. Whether or not the Halo games are the epitome of originality or not, who cares? Just as with my movies, I want my video games to be rampant escapism with an overdose of adrenaline. If I'm vicariously thrown into scenarios that just happen to be reminiscent of favorite SF movies, and lots of things explode, then all the better!

While science fiction can be used to examine the human condition and to make social commentary—the original *Star Trek*, *Starship Troopers*, and even *Battlestar Galactica* v. 2.0 are excellent examples here—science fiction can also serve as unbridled escapism. The viewer or reader or game player—the participant—isn't preoccupied with day-to-day problems if the story successfully transports him to distant worlds or future times. Of course, the participant has a role in this as well. It is the duty of the author to create a situation interesting enough to be worthy of the time invested in a visit, but it is incumbent upon the participant to be amenable to be taken on the journey. The term is "willing suspension of disbelief," originally coined by Samuel Coleridge in 1817.

Fans of science fiction media willingly allow ourselves to believe that the *Enterprise* can transport people by converting them to energy and subsequently reconstructing them, that *Galactica* has artificial gravity, and that the *Millennium Falcon* can, in fact, make the Kessel run in less than twelve parsecs. We accept a measure of unproven (faster-than-light travel), or even highly implausible (light sabers), science and technology if it's interwoven with a ripping good yarn. At the same time, if the science fiction work includes too many obvious technical gaffes—especially if they are easily circumvented and the story equally as entertaining if done accurately—the participant is "taken out" of the story, suspension of disbelief itself suspended, and the dramatic impact lessened or lost. With millions of computers in service today, coupled with the accessibility of the Internet, we have an increasingly tech-savvy population: a population that largely appreciates technical accuracy in stories and which, more to the point, notices when things are amiss. To this end, Hollywood is increasingly using technical advisors in science fiction television and cinema to ensure that the science part of science fiction is depicted as accurately as possible and that the audience stays within the action.

If the universe, characters, or story is particularly compelling, one might choose to wander that universe of his or her own accord. The Internet is full of bulletin boards where members compare and contrast the capabilities of the Viper Mark II with the Mark VIII, or debate whether or not they would take the blue pill or the red one. Of course, this is just a high-tech version of science fiction fellowship and escapism that has already existed at science fiction conventions for decades. Succinctly put, it can be fun to play in somebody else's sandbox. The *Halo* universe, detailed in the video games, novels, and upcoming movie, is a richly detailed one and lends itself well to such musings. An entire book could be written about the science and physics, both explicit and implied, within the *Halo* universe, but with only a little scientific knowledge we can have a lot of fun simply musing about a spinning ringed megastructure—suspended between a planet and its moon—that doubles as a research facility and a superweapon.

This Is the Way the World...Begins

The term "megastructure" refers to a huge artificial structure for which one of its three special dimensions is 100 kilometers or greater. Both SF and speculative science have contemplated large-scale constructs for years, such as the Dyson Sphere and *Star Trek*'s Borg Unimatrix; even the planet Earth, as represented in *The Hitchhiker's Guide to the Galaxy*, would qualify. The first literary use of a ring-shaped megastructure occurred in Larry Niven's 1970 Hugo and Nebula award-winning novel *Ringworld*. Niven elaborates on the details of such a Ringworld, also known as a Niven Ring, in his 1974 book *A Hole in Space*:

> I myself have dreamed up an intermediate step between Dyson Spheres and planets. Build a ring 93 million miles in radius—one Earth orbit—which would make it 600 million miles long. If we have the mass of Jupiter to work with, and if we make it 1,000 miles wide, we get a thickness of about a thousand meters. The Ringworld would thus be much sturdier than a Dyson Sphere.

Although Forerunner Halos are also huge ring-shaped habitats, they are comparatively smaller by several orders of magnitude: the radii of the Halo megastructures are a "mere" 5,000 kilometers—more similar to Earth's average radius, 6,371 kilometers, than that of a Ringworld. In fact, because the Halos we have seen to date orbit gas giant planets instead of encircling stars, they are less ring *worlds* than they are ring *satellites*.

A 5,000 kilometer radius would yield a circumference of roughly 31,400 kilometers. If the Halos had a width-to-radius ratio similar to that of Niven's Ringworld, they would be approximately 5.37 kilometers wide. They are significantly wider, though, at 320 kilometers. The Halos, then, would have a surface area of 10 million square kilometers—slightly larger than the surface area of Canada, and approximately 2 percent of the surface area of Earth. Of course, since we know that there are lakes, seas, and rivers on the Halos, the livable surface area would be fractionally less.

What raw materials would it take to construct a Halo, and in what quantities? In order to determine the amount of raw materials required, and what elements may exist in the necessary abundances, we first must calculate the volume of the structure. While a Halo is proportionally wider than a Niven Ring, it is thicker in absolute measure. Niven proposed that a Ringworld be 1 kilometer thick, whereas the Halos are quite a bit sturdier at 22.3 kilometers thick. The total volume of a Halo would be roughly 224 million cubic kilometers, a bit more than 0.02 percent of the volume of Earth.

Of what would a Halo be composed, then? Almost since the genre began, science fiction authors have resorted to the invention of new and exotic materials to endow their structures/spacecraft/armor with the desired combinations of weight, strength, and other material properties. The practice is so common that a term has even been coined for fictitious substances that have such improbable combinations of material properties: unobtanium. If we dare to imagine how a Halo might plausibly be built, one constraint must be that we shy away from unobtanium and consider only materials that exist in practical abundances in the real universe. In the book *Halo: Fall of Reach*, however, spectroscopic analysis of the composition of Installation 04 is "inconclusive," which seems to imply quite strongly that the Halos are, in fact, composed of unobtanium. Let's go out on a limb, then, and assume that the Halos have a thin outer protective sheath composed of a super-strong, heretofore unknown, alloy that envelopes an internal structure composed of more universal elements.

Iron, in addition to being the principle component of the cores of terrestrial—or Earth-like—planets (Mercury, Venus, Earth, and Mars), is also common in asteroids. In fact, in the solar system many asteroids are composed almost entirely of iron and nickel. Carbon is a fairly common element as well. Then it would be a reasonable assumption that the primary Halo structure is composed of steel—which is an alloy of iron and carbon—with perhaps other elements in smaller amounts. Although less universally abundant, nickel and magnesium, also common in steel, exist in amounts abundant enough to create a very strong and comparatively light steel alloy.

We now know the approximate volume of a Halo and the density of its principle component (a reasonable average density for steel is 7.7 grams per cubic centimeter). Normally, these values would be enough to calculate its approximate mass. We need still one more quantity, though. Views of the exterior surfaces of Installations 04 and 05 clearly reveal direct-vision ports (read: windows) and what appear to be docking hatches. The obvious implication is that the inner surface of the ring is not the only habitable portion of a Halo—obviously a fraction of the ring structure itself is hollow and used for living space, laboratories, even the hardware, maintenance, and pulse generator spaces for the Halo's weaponry. If we assume that the primary ring structure is roughly 50 percent empty space, then we end up with a total mass of a Halo of about 1.7×10^{17} kilograms, or 1,700 million billion kilograms.

In *A Hole in Space*, Larry Niven calculates that it would take the mass of Jupiter to build his Ringworld. A major complication, however, is that jovian, or Jupiter-like, planets represent the bulk of the mass of a planetary system like ours, yet they are composed largely of very light materials such as hydrogen and helium. Each has several Earth masses worth of solid material (rock and metals) at their core, but the sum total of all the rock and metal in the solar system—that of the inner planets, the asteroids, the jovian planets, and moons—would equal less than one-sixth of one Jupiter's mass worth of potential construction materials. The mass calculated for a Halo is approximately twice the mass of Ceres (the largest asteroid in the solar system's Asteroid Belt), a bit less than the Pluto's moon Charon, or the mass of a sphere of solid iron roughly 57 kilometers in radius. The entire asteroid belt between Mars and Jupiter would have just about enough mass to construct one Halo.

The Neighborhood: A Halo's Place in Space

Though it is likely that Halos heretofore unseen may exist in different environments, Installations 04 and 05 were both in orbit around jovian planets. In *Halo: Combat Evolved*, Installation 04 orbits the superjovian gas planet Threshold (Earth Survey Catalog B1008-AG), which, in turn, orbits the star Soell. Like Jupiter, Threshold is a gas giant with clouds of ammonia (white) and ammonium hydrosulfide (reddish brown) crystals. Unlike Jupiter, though, the diameter of Threshold is given at 214,604 kilometers, exactly half again as large as Jupiter (it is unlikely this is a coincidence, more likely a conscious choice on the part of the game designers).

The *Halo* game designers have exhibited an amazing attention to detail throughout the games. It is therefore likely that this is a result of recent astronomical discoveries more than any other reason, but jovian planets like Threshold are unlikely to exist in the real universe. Jupiter is about as large as a jovian planet can be. If increasingly more mass were added to Jupiter, it would begin to contract, collapsing under its own weight—becoming smaller even as it increased in mass. If a gas planet the size of Threshold did exist, and it had approximately Jupiter's density, it would "weigh in" at a bit less than 3.8 Jupiter masses, or around 1,070 Earth masses. In reality, though, an object of 3.8 Jupiter masses would be smaller than Jupiter, while an object the radius of Threshold would be a medium-sized brown dwarf.

Jupiter

IMAGE COURTESY OF NASA/JPL-CALTECH

The debate of the late 1990s and early 2000s regarding Pluto's status as a planet was less about Pluto than it was the definition of the cut-off point of what defines a planet at the low-mass end of the spectrum. A cut-off for the high-mass end of the spectrum has been in existence for quite some time, however. Large planets, like stars, tend to be composed largely of hydrogen. If an object has enough mass to sustain the nuclear fusion of hydrogen, thus generating its own light and heat, it is considered a star. To sustain hydrogen fusion and become a star, a body has to have roughly eighty-four Jupiter masses or more. Objects between twelve and eighty-four Jupiter masses have properties that are intermediate between jovian planets and the smallest red dwarf stars and are called brown dwarfs. Although theoretically predicted to exist back in the 1960s, the first confirmed brown dwarf was viewed in 1995 and is 400 light years away from Earth in the Pleiades (a.k.a Subaru) open star cluster. Known as Teide 1, it is roughly twice the diameter of Jupiter, yet has fifty-five times Jupiter's mass. For Threshold's rasois to be 1.5 Jupiter radii, it would likely have at least twenty Jupiter masses of material and would appear quite differently—it would be more uniform in appearance than a jovian planet, as opposed to having multi-colored cloud bands.

Installation 05, or the Delta Halo from *Halo 2*, orbits the gas giant planet Substance. Less information is given about Substance than for Threshold, but based on its color, it is likely more Uranus- or Neptune-like than Jupiter-like. Uranus and Neptune are both blue, or bluish-green, in color, suggesting the presence of methane in their atmospheres. Methane absorbs the red light from the sun, and the resultant reflected

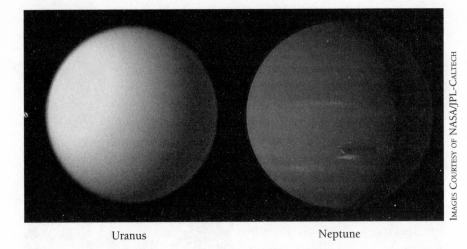

Uranus   Neptune

IMAGES COURTESY OF NASA/JPL-CALTECH

light appears blue. So, we can make a logical deduction regarding the substance of Substance simply by its color.

Not only is Threshold unusual in that it appears to have properties of both a jovian planet and a small star, it is also unusual in that it has only one moon, and a very large one at that. Known gas giants have numerous moons, most of them small. By way of example, at present count, Jupiter has sixty-three moons, and Saturn has forty-eight. Even if some, even most, of the moons of Threshold had been used as construction materials for Installation 04, it is unlikely they all would have been suitable. Most natural satellites of jovian planets, especially those as distant from their sun as Threshold appears to be, are composed of a mixture of ice and rock. In fact, it is normally so cold where the gas giants live that planetary scientists consider ice to be a rock—because ice is a main component of many of the solid objects in the outer solar system, and at the temperatures that exist in the outer solar system, ice is normally as hard as granite. Given that metals are comparatively rare around gas giants, it is unlikely that all of the moons would have been used as Halo construction materials. Perhaps some were melted for lakes, and some processed for atmosphere, but this still does not entirely explain the dearth of moons around such a large planet.

A likely explanation is that the region around Threshold was cleared on purpose. Alpha Halo Monitor 343 Guilty Spark claims that Installation 04 is at least 101,217 years old. While that represents the blink of an eye in the cosmic timescale, it is still enough time for the Halo to have accumulated numerous impact scars, a few quite large. While the bulk of material in a planetary system is swept up and accreted as part of the planet-formation process, there are still countless small—and not-so-small—particles careening through the system. When the Hubble Space Telescope (HST) was serviced by the space shuttle Atlantis in 2002, it had literally hundreds of micrometeoroid impacts. In fact, it has been estimated that every square meter of HST receives five impacts from sand-grain-sized particles every year. Most impactors are small, some aren't: there was a three-quarter-inch hole in HST as well. After a span of 100,000 years, a megastructure the size of a Halo would be scoured and likely would have suffered a major impact event or two. This would be catastrophic, since a major impact would likely release as much energy as was released at the end of the game by the fusion drive on *Pillar of Autumn*, and we know what happened there. Even the claim that the Halo had some sort of force field is inconsistent with what we've seen: human and Covenant spacecraft seemed to have no resistance in coming (both landing and crashing) and going. Given all that we've seen, then, it may very well be that the Forerunners found a way to clear the Threshold system of debris to ensure the safety of Installation 04 and its research.

The exception, of course, is Threshold's lone enigmatic moon, named Basis. Basis is unusual by solar system standards. It's a huge moon. With a radius of 11,924 kilometers, it is nearly twice the radius of the planet Earth and has over 6.5 times the volume! Just as there was a bit of a discrepancy with Threshold's planet/brown dwarf duality, a similar statement can be made for Basis. Giant planets like Threshold radiate a lot of energy, especially infra-red energy. This means that although the light and heat from Soell is quite faint, it's nevertheless quite toasty near a body like Threshold. This would imply that Basis is composed primarily of rock, like Jupiter's innermost large moon, Io. Because of Threshold's heat, icy satellites would not remain icy long. On the other hand, if we assume that Basis is, in fact, composed of rock, and if it had a density close to that of Io (which is still less than that for any of the terrestrial planets), then the gravity on the surface would be nearly 1.2 times that of Earth. Master Chief and his fellow Marines might be moving a trifle slowly on Basis if this were the case. The gravity on Basis appears to be similar to that for Earth, however, and it would certainly be enough to hold an atmosphere. Further, the appearance of Basis is not dissimilar to Jupiter's moon Europa. If we assume that Basis has a similar composition as Europa, and we assume the same density, then it has the same gravity as Earth (this, perhaps, is what the game designers had in mind). It seems, then, that Basis is a bit of a paradox. For gravity there to be the same as Earth, the moon would almost certainly have to be composed of a mixture of ice and rock, but since the surface seems to have a temperature comfortable to humans, then most of that ice should be in the liquid state.

A careful examination of the viewscreen on *Pillar of Autumn* shows that Installation 04 is halfway between Threshold and Basis. This is an untenable place to put a Halo for many reasons. More likely the Halo is situated near, or orbiting about, the L1 Lagrange point between Threshold and Basis, which would put it closer to Basis and not at the halfway point. In a system with two massive bodies (like Threshold and Basis, which we'll call the primary and secondary bodies), there are five points where a third body of negligible mass, owing to a combination of gravitational attraction and orbital *centrifugal force* (understanding that centrifugal force is what physicists call a fictitious force; here, the more colloquial usage is adopted), would remain stationary with respect to the two massive bodies. These are known as LaGrange points, and they are labeled L1 through L5. The L4 and L5 points, sixty degrees ahead and behind the smaller massive body in the same orbit, are stable. Objects placed in a co-planar orbit at either L4 or L5 will remain in roughly the same location relative to the two massive objects. The solar system is, in fact, full of examples. At the Sun/Jupiter L4 and L5 points are hundreds of asteroids, called the Trojan Asteroids, which co-orbit with Jupiter. The Saturnian moon Tethys even has smaller moons at its L4 (Telesto) and L5 (Calypso) points.

The L1, L2, and L3 points are called *meta-stable*, however. All three points orbit the primary at the same orbital rate as does the secondary body, and each maintains the same relative position between the two. L1 is along the line connecting the primary body to the secondary body and is situated at what a mathematician would call a *saddle point*. A ball bearing placed on a saddle would roll to the middle of the saddle from front to back but would have a tendency to roll off to one side or the other. The L1 point is stable in one direction (along the primary-secondary line) but unstable along its orbit, hence meta-stable. This implies that Installation 04 actively corrects its orbit to keep Threshold

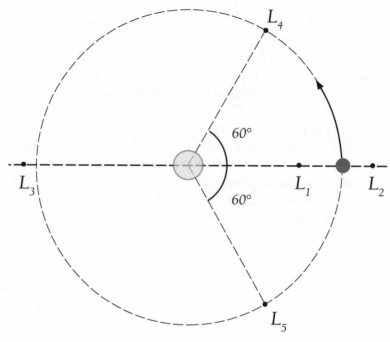

Figure 1

and Basis at the same relative locations. Though the L1 point is unstable, there exist trajectories that *orbit* the L1 point that are stable. The NASA Solar and Heliospheric Observatory (SOHO) and Genesis missions, both of which took data about the sun, were on such trajectories (which, ironically, are called *halo orbits*).

In placing a structure like a Halo so near a body like Threshold, other complications arise. One would be the radiation environment. The largest structure in the solar system is the magnetic environment around the planet Jupiter. If it could actually be seen, from Earth it would appear to be a few times larger than the full moon. Such a large and intense magnetic field traps charged subatomic particles like electrons, which spiral along the magnetic field lines. Some electrons can even be accelerated to relativistic speeds—a large fraction of the speed of light. This makes life near a jovian planet difficult at best. A human standing on Jupiter's innermost large moon, Io, would receive a lethal dose of radiation from only a few minute's worth of exposure. Surely the radiation environment surrounding a Halo in close orbit about a gas giant would be similar.

Earth is bathed in a stream of changed subatomic particles not dissimilar to those in close proximity to Jupiter: the solar wind. Earth is protected from charged particles where Io is not, owing to its magnetic field. Since electrons and other charged particles are deflected by magnetic fields, the solar wind flows around Earth, except at the poles. At Earth's poles, there is a hole, or cusp, in the magnetic field where the solar wind can penetrate more deeply. The solar wind's interaction with Earth's upper atmosphere underneath the polar cusps is what creates the aurorae.

Certainly a Halo bathed in the radiation of a gas giant like Threshold would require shielding similar to that around Earth, and it turns out that to do this might be a fairly straightforward task. Magnetic fields are generated by moving charged particles like electrons, implying that any wire along which a current flows is surrounded by a magnetic field. It's not inconceivable, then, that huge conductive cables could run the entire 31,416-kilometer circumference of a Halo, nestled within the ring structure itself. By creating electrical currents within these cables, the Forerunners could have easily created a protective magnetic environment that was strong enough to make a Halo inhabitable, but not so strong that it would interfere with the function of electronic equipment.

One Spinning Ring to Rule Them All

After our brief wandering through a Halo's space, let's make a closer examination. What is life like, and what are some implications of life on a planet-sized spinning metal ring? Altough it is established in the *Halo* universe that the Forerunners, Covenant, and even humans have some degree of artificial gravity generation technology, gravity on a Halo is largely simulated by centrifugal force. Since modern-day science knows no way to generate gravity artificially, a very common technique used in both literary (e.g. *Ringworld, Rendezvous with Rama*) and cinematic (e.g., *Mission to Mars, 2001: A Space Odyssey*) science fiction is to use the centrifugal force of a spinning ring or cylindrical structure to simulate gravity. More germane to this topic, Larry Niven describes how gravity would be simulated on a Ringworld:

> There are other advantages. We can spin it for gravity. A rotation on its axis of 770 miles/second would give the Ringworld one gravity outward.

The apparent gravity on Installations 04 and 05 is close to that of Earth. For a Halo with a radius of 5,000 kilometers to simulate one Earth gravity, it would have to spin with a tangential speed of slightly more than seven kilometers per second. That implies that the Halo would rotate once every hour and fifteen minutes, or 19¼ times a day.

The concepts of day and night would, therefore, take on entirely different meanings on a Halo than they do on Earth. For that matter, they would even be entirely different than that for Niven's Ringworld. In Niven's novels, the Ringworld has "shadow squares," almost a mini Ringworld, encircling the central star at a smaller radius:

> Set up an inner ring of shadow squares—light orbiting structures to block out part of the sunlight—and we can have day-and-night cycles in whatever period we like.

The shadow squares are connected with thin but extremely strong filament. By alternately passing and obscuring light, the shadow squares simulate day and night—the size of both the shadow squares and their interstices dictating the duration of each. The orientation in space of a Halo would determine what percentage of each rotation would receive both sunlight and shadow; however, if Halos orbit their gas giant in the equatorial plane, as it appears they do in the game, then a Halo goes into eclipse periodically as well. While there exist tilted, or inclined, orbits that never go into eclipse, by virtue of the fact that we can see that Installation 04 orbits between Threshold and Basis, it is not in one of these orbits. Given the stated size of Threshold, and the apparent distance to Basis, it is likely that Installation 04 would be plunged into complete darkness at least once every Earth day.

An object—a soldier, an Elite, a Scorpion MBT, a Warthog recon vehicle, anything—in direct contact with the surface of the ring would perceive the centrifugal force to be the equivalent of gravity. Anything not in direct contact would tend to follow basic laws of dynamics, but laws that might seem counter-intuitive at first. On the second level of *Halo: Combat Evolved* (a level called "Halo," in fact), Master Chief can see a waterfall shortly after making ring-fall. Figure 2 shows the results of computer simulations of the trajectory of one drop of water over the waterfall if it were subject to Earth's gravity, and the trajectory of one drop of water on a Halo—assuming that the waterfall is 305 meters (1,000 feet) high and oriented along the Halo's spin direction. We see

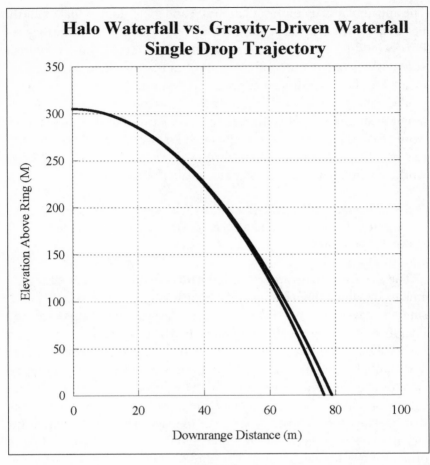

Figure 2

that a drop would fall two meters farther on a Halo than on Earth. That's not a great difference, but if the water flow were oriented perpendicular to the spin direction, it would deflect two meters to the side, which would look odd for somebody used to viewing terrestrial waterfalls.

The ring's spin would have an even more pronounced effect on objects with a longer time of flight. While most of the combat in *Halo* takes place at close range, let's assume we want to use our M808B Scorpion Main Battle Tank, which fires hypervelocity rounds, as a piece of artillery and fire projectiles at a much greater distance. Entry-level physics students learn about trajectories—that the trajectory of a projectile fired from a cannon takes the shape of a parabola (actually, an ellipse,

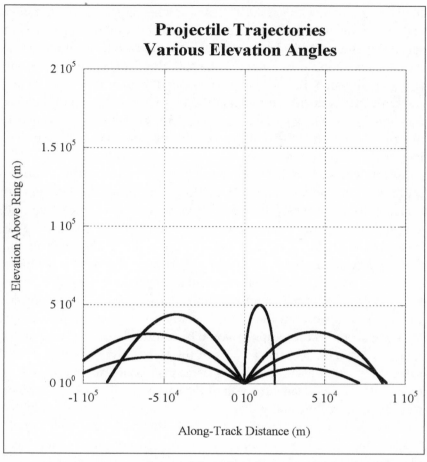

Figure 3

since the trajectory represents a partial orbit). In the absence of wind, a round fired straight up will return straight down and completely ruin the day of whosoever fired it. Long-range trajectories on a Halo would be quite different.

Figure 3 shows the results of computer simulations of long-range trajectories of rounds fired from the inside surface of a 5,000-kilometer ring spinning at nineteen times per day. The assumed muzzle velocity was 1,000 meters per second. Figure 3 shows the trajectories for initial barrel elevations of thirty, forty-five, sixty, and ninety degrees above local "horizontal," both in the direction of the ring rotation (+X) and in the direction counter to the ring rotation (-X). We can see that a round fired straight up does *not*, in fact, return to where it was fired, but rather eighteen kilometers downrange due to the seven kilometers per second speed that the round had before it was even fired. Note a marked asymmetry between projectiles fired in the spin direction as opposed to the anti-spin direction. Rounds fired in the spin direction have a greater initial horizontal velocity, and impact the ring sooner than those fired in the direction opposite to the ring's spin. A rocket fired from a launcher, or a projectile from a fuel rod gun, would suffer similar deflections if it had to travel long range.

Targeting distant objects for living combatants would be counter-intuitive on a ring where centrifugal force substitutes for gravity. Automated fire control systems would have to determine, then take into account for targeting calculations, the orientation of the weapon with respect to the Halo. There is actually a hint of this in the game. In the first *Halo* game, the assault rifle has a "compass" that always points to the planet Threshold. If the ring's orientation is known (and this might be a simple calibration), then it would be fairly easy for a microprocessor to take into account the ring's spin when targeting. So, long-range targeting for projectile weapons would be counter-intuitive. Some of the weapons available to Master Chief in the *Halo* universe are, however, Covenant particle beam weapons: plasma pistols and plasma rifles. Particle beams travel at large fraction of the speed of light. A beam of light would transverse the entire diameter of a Halo in thirty-three milliseconds, and a particle beam would take only slightly longer. So a particle beam simply does not have time to undergo the deflection of a projectile—where the weapon is pointed is where the damage will occur.

Another situation for which interaction with a Halo might initially prove counter-intuitive occurs when a spacecraft attempts to land upon/dock with the installation. Clearly seen on both Installations 04 and 05 are what appear to be docking ports on the exterior surface of the ring. This would obviate the need for any atmospheric entry procedures, but as we shall discuss briefly, even the atmosphere is less a problem than it would be for a planet. A craft approaching a Halo from the exterior face of the ring would have to "fall in step" with its seven kilometers-per-second rotation rate, while also taking into account the curved exterior surface. At that speed, and at that distance from the Halo's central spin axis, the craft would undergo a constant outward force of approximately one Earth gravity. At the same time, if there was a pilot error or the craft lost power for whatever reason, an approach from the exterior might prove to be the safest way to dock with a Halo—the constant centrifugal force means that most conceivable errors would cause the craft to be thrown clear of the ring, instead of crashing into it.

Approaching a Halo's inner surface would, in some respects, be far less complicated than approaching a planet or a moon, but attempting to land on a Halo's inner surface would be significantly more problematic. Although it is established that the Forerunners had artificial gravity generation technology, it doesn't seem that this comes into play when landing on a Halo. Not only does a Halo structure have a fairly small mass, even compared to a small moon, but the mass is evenly distributed radially. The craft would therefore feel a gravitational tug, albeit small, from all segments of the ring. Succinctly, since a Halo has a trivial amount of gravity, a spacecraft could approach a Halo and comfortably sit within its circumference as the ring rotated around it.

Approaching the inner ring surface would be the tough part. Although a craft could sit essentially immobile as the ring spun around it, recall that the ring is spinning at seven kilometers per second. That equates to 4.45 miles/second, or roughly 15,660 miles per hour (by comparison, the equator of Earth is moving at rather pedestrian 1,670 kilometers per hour, or 1,037 miles per hour). To minimize the relative motion, a craft landing on the interior of the ring would have to similarly move a speed of, or close to, seven kilometers per second—under nearly 1G of acceleration—while slowly moving outwards from the ring's spin axis. Just as any pilot error/malfunction/power outage on a craft approaching the ring from the exterior would be minimized by the tendency of the centrifugal force to throw the craft away from the ring, the same force on a craft approaching from the inside would tend to throw it against a ring moving at twenty-one times the speed of sound.

Of course, for there to be sound, there has to be an atmosphere. Larry Niven describes how this is possible on a Ringworld:

> We wouldn't even have to roof it over. Put walls a thousand miles high at each rim, aimed at the sun, and very little air will leak over the edges.

It turns out that walls a fraction of that size (though higher than they appear in the game) would hold in enough of an atmosphere to make a Halo habitable, but that same atmosphere might represent a danger to craft attempting to land. If the craft is in a spiral trajectory—revolving around the Halo spin axis at the same rate the ring spins—lowering itself slowly onto the ring, there is little problem. Friction with the atmosphere would be minimal and, in fact, in this instance there would be less re-entry heating than a craft would experience approaching a planet like Earth. If the spacecraft/ring relative velocity were not nullified, a craft on approach to a Halo would suddenly find itself subject to air friction—resulting in both intense heat and shear—of a supersonic airflow. While there would certainly be shear in a Halo atmosphere due to the ring's rotation, and the upper layers of air would not be moving at near the speed as that near the surface, without the proper approach, a ship attempting to land on the inner surface of a Halo could still be met with near-instantaneous incineration—not a particularly welcoming introduction.

Only the Beginning?

A physics professor once said to me, "Any topic, studied in sufficient detail, becomes infinitely complex." Here we've merely skimmed the cream of the richness of science, explicit and implied, of the *Halo* universe. As suggested earlier, an entire book could, and perhaps should, be written about the subject. We've discussed weaponry very little, and haven't even covered issues like the wind and weather on a Halo. My post-planetarium show dinner companions might, in fact, be both appalled and delighted that such entertaining intellectual musings could find their genesis in a video game where lots of things explode.

Kevin R. Grazier, Ph.D., is currently the science advisor for the Sci-Fi Channel series *Eureka* and *Battlestar Galactica*, as well as the PBS animated series *The Zula Patrol*. He also writes the more-or-less monthly *Battlestar Galactica TECH Blog* on hollywoodnorthreport. com. Dr. Grazier works at NASA's Jet Propulsion Laboratory (JPL) in Pasadena, California, and holds the dual titles of investigation scientist and science planning engineer for the Cassini/Huygens Mission to Saturn and Titan. He has won both JPL- and NASA-wide awards. Dr. Grazier completed his undergraduate and MS degrees at Purdue University. His doctoral research at UCLA was in planetary physics: long-term, large-scale computer simulations of solar system dynamics, evolution, and chaos. He continues this research with collaborators at UCLA, Los Alamos National Laboratory, the University of Auckland, Purdue University, and the Space Science Institute. Dr. Grazier is also very active in bringing the wonders of science and space to the public. Through various outreach programs, he speaks to thousands of K–12 students every year and serves on two NASA educational product review panels. He teaches classes in basic astronomy, planetary science, cosmology, and the search for extraterrestrial life at UCLA, Santa Monica College, and/or Glendale College. Dr. Grazier has been featured in several documentaries, co-hosted the premier episode of Discovery Channel's *Science Live! Kid's Edition*, and even co-anchored CNN's coverage of Cassini's Saturn orbit insertion. He is also a planetarium lecturer at L.A.'s famed Griffith Observatory and at the Drescher Planetarium at Santa Monica College. Dr. Grazier lives in Sylmar, California, and, occasionally, Mesa, Arizona.

REFERENCES

Britt, Robert Roy. "How Hubble Has Survived a Decade of Impacts." *Space. com.* 26 Feb. 2002. <http://www.space.com/scienceastronomy/astronomy/hubble_impact_020226.html>.

Niven, Larry. "Bigger than Worlds," from *A Hole in Space*. Ballantine Books, 1974.

——. *Ringworld*. Ballantine Books, 1970.

Nyland, Eric. *Halo: The Fall of Reach*. Del Rey Books, 2001.

The Halopedia. <http://halo.wikia.com>.

Halo: Combat Evolved. Bungie Studios. Microsoft Game Studios. 15 Nov. 2001. Xbox.

Halo 2. Bungie Studios. Microsoft Game Studios. 9 Nov. 2004. Xbox.

Tired of playing Halo? *Create a blockbuster film instead.*

Glenna Whitley

LIGHTS, CAMERA, PLAY!

ALEX WINN'S BEDROOM was crammed with a dozen teenagers. The smells of old pizza, rank sneakers, and sweat hung in the sweltering air. Empty boxes of Goldfish crackers littered the floor and peeked from under the rumpled bed. Against one wall, emitting incredible heat and a blue glow, stood a bank of televisions, computer monitors, and three or four Xboxes, all networked together to play *Halo 2*. Three fans buzzed in the corners.

Boys and girls were draped over each other like puppies on the bed, on chairs, on the floor, staring intently at the screens. All had game controllers in their hands and were manipulating them furiously to put their "actors" through their paces.

Armor-covered warriors could be seen on the monitors crouching, raising their guns, shooting, running, jumping, more shooting. Aliens shooting back. Then an explosion: *KA-boooom! KA-blaaaaaam! Aaau-uughh!* Five enemies of humankind bite the dust.

Later they dubbed the voices: the "voice of God" intonation of the Praetor; the snide drone of the Cleric; the lighter female voice of tough Special Forces Commander Anda Sofadee. Close to midnight, they had one scene down and several dozen to go. Everyone left to do their homework—they were all students at Highland Park High School—and grab a few hours of sleep.

Except Winn. He stayed up a few more hours to edit and add music. The group faced a tight deadline to post their last episode of *The Codex Series* on the Internet. Winn was exhausted, physically and mentally. They'd been working on the project every waking moment they weren't in school or at work for ten months. In just a few days, Winn was leaving to start his freshman year at the University of Southern California. Most of his cohorts were leaving for college as well, but they couldn't disappoint their fans.

At midnight on Friday, August 13, 2005, Ryan Luther uploaded the last episode of *The Codex* to the Web site he'd created. Their server was slammed by fans in the United States, Sweden, China, and Korea—anywhere in the world where gamers lived and breathed *Halo 2*. They got one million hits in a week, and the praise rolled in.

The following Monday, Winn left for USC, and the others scattered to three different time zones. Their movie—their 109-minute *machinima*—was finally finished.

For those who don't know, which includes almost everybody outside the small subculture of aficionados, the word machinima is a combination of *machine* and *cinema*.

The phrase was coined about ten years ago to describe movies made using a computer game such as *Quake*. After writing a script, players manipulate the game's characters to act out scenes, which they digitally record and then edit, dub voices and sounds, and score the action just like film. Some games allow modification of the characters and game's environment; others don't. Some machinima works stick to the story line of the game. Others veer off wildly into new scenarios.

As computer graphics for games grow more sophisticated, some fans believe machinima will revolutionize filmmaking. *Wired* magazine Editor-in-Chief Chris Anderson has called machinima "basement Pixar," a way for anyone to make low-cost movies with animation. "The technology is exponentially developing," says Paul Marino, a 3D animator who in 2002 founded the nonprofit Academy of Machinima Arts and Sciences in New York. "People are starting to see this as a way to do production. Television is interested in machinima because it cuts down on production costs. The History Channel used [the World War II game] *Brothers in Arms* 2 to explore some narratives. There's been a lot of interest in Hollywood."

Last year, Marino moderated a panel on machinima at the Sundance Film Festival. "I guess we've arrived," he says.

It's the millions of gamers who will be at the forefront of the machinima revolution, if it happens. They're the ones willing to spend long hours manipulating the characters in games and exploring the niches and glitches that can be exploited for exciting scenes. And they understand how involved fellow gamers can become with their favorite characters. "It's even more emotional than the movies," Winn says, "because it feels like it's happening to you."

It's a world most parents don't understand and, in some ways, fear. They worry their offspring are playing games that are too violent, too gory, too amoral. What kinds of machinima could teenagers make with *Grand Theft Auto* or *Hitman: Blood Money*?

Relax, parents. That kid who spends days in his room blasting alien life forms could be the next Peter Jackson, who, by the way, is exec-producing a movie based on *Halo*.

The parents of the rest of the core group that created *The Codex*—Ryan Luther, Meghan Foster, and Patrick Malone—knew their teenagers were at the Winns, but most didn't understand what they were doing. Making a "machinima" film? Huh?

Luther's mom assumed it was one more way her son could waste time in the alternate universe of online games, which he'd been obsessed with for years. She'd once put a lock on their computer. He picked it.

Foster's mom worried that her daughter had slipped off the wagon. At the beginning of her junior year at Highland Park, Foster had been playing an online role-playing game so compulsively her mom had removed the computer from her bedroom.

Becky Winn, a writer, was lukewarm. She thought her son Alex, a budding filmmaker, should have been writing his college application essays.

And it was safe to say that Malone's parents weren't thrilled; when *Halo 2* came out, Malone had stayed up for three days to play.

But no one was more stunned than the teenagers when *The Codex* became an international sensation on the Internet, getting 3 million hits in one week and not just from *Halo* players. A month after the last episode was released, *Wired's* Anderson raved about it in his online diary after his elementary-age kids showed it to him.

"My children's favorite film was not made by Disney," Anderson wrote on September 29, "but by a dozen Dallas teenagers playing a video game in one of their parents' basement." Well, he got the room wrong, but no matter.

In his online diary, thelongtail.com, Anderson called *The Codex* the best machinima he'd ever seen, with a "stirring plot... edge-of-your-seat pacing, distinctive characters and a pulse-quickening soundtrack.... I'm on my third viewing myself, and I must say that Episode 18 is a stunner, a masterful interweaving of simultaneous rally-the-troops speeches by commanders about to battle. It builds to a crescendo that will leave you breathless."

Quentin Tarantino would have killed for a review like that when he was eighteen.

Luther and Winn took the long and elaborate *Halo* plot and created a script with their own characters. *The Codex* tells the story of a battle between humans and a group of aliens called the Covenant on the planet Ariaos II. The Covenant, led by the Praetor, invade in an attempt to find the Codex, an ancient structure created by a long-gone race called the Forerunners. Gaining control of the Codex will allow the Covenant troops to activate super-weapons known as "Halos," which will destroy life in the galaxy. (Why would the Covenant want to do that? It's a religious thing. Go figure.) The Spartans, human soldiers, must find the Codex first and destroy it.

For non-players, watching the movie is, at first, confusing; the soldiers wear helmets and, except for the color of their armor, are indistinguishable. But every episode develops the main characters, each with a unique voice, and as it builds, it sucks you in. There's power-grabbing, duty, betrayal, sassy feminism, courage, a bit of romance, the cynicism of grunts, and lots of blasting away with loud weapons. The score deftly weaves together music and sound to build and release tension. Most important, by the end, you care who wins.

Now *The Codex* creators get recognized by peers on their college campuses and at gaming conferences. They're selling *Codex* T-shirts, giving away DVDs and CDs of their soundtrack to sponsors, and running a forum for people who want to discuss the movie. Their success is all the more amazing when you realize most machinima makers are in their twenties and thirties, not teenagers.

"It's a testament to machinima," says Marino, the author of *3D Game-Based Filmmaking: The Art of Machinima.* "These young kids who had a great idea for a series had the tools to do it. It's the democratization of animated filmmaking."

The seminal moment for machinima was a 1996 film called *Diary of a Camper*, made by a group of *Quake* players called the Rangers. "*Quake* came with a cool feature that allowed you to record the game, so you could share the moves you made," Marino says. "With that recording feature, this group decided to create a narrative point of view."

The film was short and silent, the story slim: The Rangers encountered a lone gunman and had to go get him. "It became hugely popular among the gaming community," Marino says.

At the time, Marino was living in New York, doing computer animation for television, a laborious and time-consuming process. "It can take hours and hours to create," Marino says. "With games it's all real-time. It takes a more live-action approach. It was logical the technologies would meet."

In 1998, Marino and his fellow *Quake* players—the ILL Clan—made a machinima called *Apartment Hunting*. Then people started doing it with other games, including *Unreal Tournament* and *Half-Life*. Gaming technology has advanced so much in the last three years, Marino says, that the difference is obvious on the screen. "The talent has matured," he says. "It's spreading out. It was, at first, just gamers. But machinima filmmakers are broadening. We are seeing kids, adults, homemakers, and older people."

David Diaz, a.k.a. "Bard Noir," posted his first machinima music video—based on characters he created for *Sims 2*—a year ago before he even knew what machinima was. Manager of a car rental shop in Houston, Diaz is a movie buff and fan of role-playing games. He dresses up every year as a bard for the Texas Renaissance Festival.

"The Sims games are anti-escapism at its best," Diaz says. "You create miniature virtual people. You design everything about them. The point is to see how they interact with one another. When they added the technology to record this, capturing the interaction, it opened it up."

Diaz first got attention with a machinima music video set to his fiancée's favorite Kurt Nilsen song, called "I." To the melancholy tune, a Sim (who resembles Diaz) anguishes over how to approach a pretty girl, practicing in the mirror, trying to approach her and failing.

"I was always interested in the girl who didn't know I existed," Diaz says. "I wanted to tell the story of an awkward artist trying to figure out how to talk to this girl." Of course, he gets the girl in the end.

"Broken," another of his machinima videos, is about an abusive relationship from two different perspectives, a woman with a baby and her boyfriend in prison, set to a song by Seether. Diaz posted them at Sims99.com, a host for all things Sims, and got great feedback.

Diaz has now made four machinima music videos. He and a creative team, including a casting director whose job it is to come up with interesting Sims characters, have started working on a twelve-part series inspired by TV's *Buffy the Vampire Slayer*. They have finished the scripts for half of the series. Diaz plans to e-mail files of completed episodes to his voice actors for dubbing.

In support of the art form, Marino's Academy of Machinima Arts and Sciences gives awards each year. There's machinima about everything from the Old West to World War II. And, of course, someday there will be machinima porn.

Last November, Activision, an entertainment software company that sells games such as *Quake* and *Doom*, just cut to the chase and released *The Movies*, a teen-rated game that lets players, well, make movies. "The French Democracy," a machinima short about the recent riots in France, was made using *The Movies*.

Instead of fighting it, game developers like Microsoft's Bungie have embraced machinima, even inserting tools into new games that make it easier. "Game developers and publishers are seeing that machinima is a way to build their brand," Marino says. "It's like a tribute to the game. It's marketing the game publishers couldn't provide. But they are playing in a dangerous space of [intellectual property] rights. If someone was packaging the DVDs and selling them, the game publishers would crack down."

The Codex Series never would have happened except for two teenage boys as different as Walt Disney and Wes Craven. Both grew up in Highland Park, are the sons of lawyers, have curly black hair and goatees, are nineteen years old and brainy. There the resemblance ends.

Ryan Luther is quiet and introverted, a loner who loves video games and has taught himself programming and Web design. He plays everything but sports games. Alexander Winn—let's just say everyone at Highland Park High School knows who he is. Tall, always wears black. Acts in school plays. Very focused. Hang with Winn for a few minutes, and you'll learn he wants to be a filmmaker.

Meghan Foster, eighteen, is a naturally pretty tomboy who looks like she'd rather slit her wrists than wear a dress. She played varsity soft-ball throughout high school and got into fencing through playing video games. Foster thrust-and-parried well enough to place third in a state-wide fencing tournament and go to the Junior Olympics. Of the four, Foster was the hard-core *Halo* fanatic, one of the only girl gamers at Highland Park High. As a senior she was taking video tech and start-ed making short films. She is now at Hollins University in Virginia and wants to major in film and sociology so she can make documentaries.

Tall and funny, Patrick Malone, eighteen, started singing and acting after someone pointed out he needed to find something to be good at other than video games. Turned out he had talent. Malone participated in various choirs at Highland Park, starred in school musicals, won solo competitions, and is now on a full-tuition scholarship to study vocal performance at Oklahoma City University.

Luther and Winn have known each other since fourth grade but re-ally became buddies in middle school at an SMU video game summer camp, which taught the basics of game design. As freshmen, Luther, Foster, and Malone were obsessively playing *Halo*, an Xbox game re-leased in 2001. "*Halo* is about a war between a coalition of alien races and humans," Winn says. "You play as this super-soldier that is trying to destroy an ancient alien weapon before the aliens can set it off. Most first-person shooters have a pretty thinly veiled plot; they're just an ex-cuse to shoot stuff. In *Halo*, it feels like a movie and has a really in-depth plot, a good back story, and good characters."

The game has spawned three novels. And it's addictive.

Malone would be up all night playing games, even in middle school. When his parents moved the computer out of his room, Malone would wait until they were asleep and sneak out to play, draping a towel over the modem so his mom and dad wouldn't hear. He hadn't bought an Xbox because he didn't think it was worth the $300 investment. His fa-ther gave him one as a gift. "I started playing *Halo* and stayed up three days doing it," Malone says. "My dad was cool with it until it affected my regular life."

When the highly anticipated *Halo 2* was released the year they were juniors, Malone camped out for four hours to buy the game. He headed home but not to grab some sleep. He played, then went to school, then missed a class because he went home to log on again.

Meghan Foster didn't even go to school that day. Probably the top female gamer in her school, a year earlier Foster had gotten so obsessed with *Everquest* that her mother had to take the computer out of her bedroom.

"I'd been up three days straight playing," Foster says. "I think what happened was I forgot to do my chores for the third week in a row. I never should have started playing *Everquest*." She now calls it "evercrack."

Why are they so into games? None of them have much insight into their addiction, but the answer is probably as easy as this: it's fun. It's competitive. And game developers have figured out how to make the quest personal. David Freeman, a consultant for games, calls it "emotioneering."

Foster became just as obsessed with *Halo*. "You become attached to the characters, your fellow Marines," she says. "It shakes you up when something happens to characters you've come to trust. A lot of people don't realize the emotional impact these things have."

Like thousands of other *Halo* addicts, Alex, Ryan, Patrick, and Meghan loved *Red vs. Blue: The Blood Gulch Chronicles*, a popular machinima comedy series based on *Halo 2*. Created by older gamers who met at the University of Texas, Austin, the series features bored futuristic soldiers enmeshed in a civil war who say stupid stuff to pass the time. Ed Halter of the *Village Voice* called it "*Clerks*-meets-*Star Wars*." Here's a sample from the first episode:

TUCKER: What are they doing?
CHURCH: What?
TUCKER: I said, what are they doing now?
CHURCH: Goddamn, I'm getting so sick of answering that question.
TUCKER: You have the fucking rifle. I can't see shit. Don't bitch at me
    because I'm not going to just sit up here and play with my dick
    all day.
CHURCH: Okay, look. They're just standing there and talking, okay?
    That's all they're doing, that's all they ever do—is just stand there
    and talk. That's what they were doing last week, that's what they
    were doing when you asked me five minutes ago. So five minutes
    from now, when you ask me "What are they doing?," my answer's
    gonna be "They're still just talkin', and they're still just standin'
    there."

The creators of *Red vs. Blue* now run a company called Rooster Teeth, based in Buda, Texas, and earn money creating machinima for commercial uses. New episodes of *Red vs. Blue*, now in its fourth season, are posted each week and downloaded by half a million people.

"*Red vs. Blue* is Beckett," says *Wired*'s Anderson. "It's doing *Waiting for Godot*. It makes an asset out of its limitations." Among the limitations: the *Halo* Marines are all wearing helmets, so they can be distinguished only by their voices. Figuring out who's who in a battle scene is difficult. And the soldiers don't have complete range of motion; for example, they are able to crouch but not sit down.

"But you can blow things up real easily," Luther says.

Red vs. Blue and its many imitators inspired Winn to think about using *Halo 2* to create a movie. He assumed that, after making short films—dealing with actors, getting location permits, coping with weather—creating machinima would be a breeze.

Winn had grown up watching old movies with his grandmother. As a teenager, he started using editing software on his computer to make trailers for real and made-up movies he'd like to see, snipping video slices and putting them to music.

The summer between his sophomore and junior year, Winn had tried making a movie based on *Ender's Game*, a popular SF book. After writing a script, Winn recruited Luther, who'd taught himself 3D modeling, and they built some ship models. Winn rounded up a cast of ten friends and twenty extras and borrowed digital video cameras from his school. He had thirty-five minutes of the story on film when Winn realized that the way he was going, the movie would be fifteen hours long. He shelved it.

"I got a half-hour into it before I realized there's a reason big-budget movies have big budgets," Winn says.

His next venture was more successful. In video tech class during his junior year, Winn was given an assignment to make a seven-minute movie with no dialogue. Winn shot an homage to old Bogart movies he'd watched with his grandmother. Filmed around Highland Park, Winn was shooting a night chase (and also acting in the scene) down an alley that dead-ended at a bank drive-through when a police car screeched up. A Dallas police officer got out, drew a gun on them, and barked, "Drop your weapons and step away from the car!"

"It was pretty scary," says Becky Winn, Alex's mother, who'd been driving a van down the alley as a camera dolly. "The officer seemed nervous."

The next night, Alex passed out fliers to residents and had two friends stand with big signs on either end of the alley: "Student Film in Progress."

Jack O'Neill, Private Detective, written, directed, and scored by Alex Winn, was accepted by a number of film festivals and won, among other prizes, a CINE Golden Eagle Award in 2004. He was the only high-school student to do so that year.

Inspired by the soundtrack of Cirque du Soleil's *Quidam*, Winn came up with the plot for another short film, bought a used digital video camera for $1,300, and recruited several teens who wanted to be actors. Shot at Love Field, "Baggage Claim" also won recognition in film festivals.

Winn realized from watching *Red vs. Blue* that recording the action through various characters' eyes was just another way of filming. But he wanted to do a feature-length drama, not a comedy.

When *Halo 2* came out, Winn and Luther explored the internal architecture of the game. "We were running on some of the multiplayer maps," Winn says. "One of the maps is a giant cave with a structure in the middle. We came up with the idea that the structure is a compendium of knowledge. Ryan came up with the idea of *The Codex*, an ancient book."

They pounded out a plot, using an undercurrent in the game that the aliens are a religious race and revere their ancients, called "Forerunners." They broke the plot into twenty episodes.

Winn—writer, director, producer—spent a week on the script for Episode 1. Luther—lead animator and voice actor for bit parts—designed their logo and Web site. They recruited Malone, a skilled actor and singer, as the male lead and Foster, the hotshot girl gamer, as the female lead. In December 2004, the core four started filming.

When Meghan Foster sat her mom down to explain why she raced to Winn's house every night after softball practice to play a video game until 10 or 11 P.M., Kathy Perry was bewildered. Foster's explanation sounded fishy, especially in light of her earlier compulsive gaming.

It was the middle of Foster's senior year in high school, and Perry thought her daughter needed to concentrate on her studies and college applications. But Perry and Meghan's father, Pete Foster, told her she could participate as long as her grades didn't suffer and she didn't miss important family events.

The students rounded up Xboxes and wired one into Winn's computer, where the view through one character's eyes would be recorded. The other Xboxes had four characters on each. Winn controlled the "camera" by moving his character with the Xbox controller and recording whatever his character saw. Instead of shooting, his character would move into a position to film the other characters, dodging bullets to get good shots, just like a war photographer. The other teens acted like puppeteers, putting their "actors" through actions to match the script.

The first few weeks were hard. "You just want to shoot and kill each other," Foster says. But the inadvertent demise of a player would mean re-shooting. They came up with a standing policy: kill an actor and get punched in the face. Accidental deaths were fewer as they got more skilled.

For battle scenes, they recruited more players. At times there'd be fifteen people in Winn's bedroom. When they were short-handed, Luther would use his bare feet on a controller.

They wanted to film at least four episodes before posting the first on the Web. But as true children of the Internet, they knew the value of pre-release hype. When a false rumor went around the *Halo* boards that something new was coming out on February 9, they decided to ride the hype.

Each of them went to various *Halo* forums and posted cryptic messages: "*The Codex* is coming!" and "On February 9 *The Codex* reveals itself," Winn wrote a poem in iambic pentameter that was supposed to sound biblical, and they posted it as an intercepted message from *The Codex*.

On February 1, Luther uploaded a short trailer on thecodexseries. com. The response melted their server: Within four hours, they'd exhausted their allotted bandwidth of 100 gigs for the month. Luther scrambled to find a Web host that would give them unlimited bandwidth, bumping their cost from $25 to $60 a month.

The trailer got great feedback except from rabid *Red vs. Blue* fans, who sneered at the upstarts. "They think if you use *Halo*, you are ripping off *Red vs. Blue*," Winn says.

On February 9, the core four and several other actors gathered at Winn's house for a launch party. In need of more puppeteers, they had pulled in Lauren Jenks, a sixteen-year-old softball player who wasn't a gamer, and taught her how to use a controller. The four were now five.

They passed out *Codex* T-shirts and held their breath while Luther uploaded the digital files of "The Gathering Storm." The episode lasted all of four minutes and twenty-six seconds.

Within a half-hour, people started posting responses on their Web site's forum that described the first episode as, in general, "awesome." Their Web host's tracking system showed they had 60,000 hits the first day; the previous day they had 12,000. Ecstatic, they turned their attention to polishing the next three episodes and starting Episode 5. By March 11, their Web site had a million hits.

They had technical trouble encoding the files and uploading them because they were so large. The footage came out too dark on some screens, which they solved by saving it in a different format. They couldn't find enough people to film a battle scene. Sometimes their own ambition—trying to make their characters do things nobody had seen in the game—made them late for their release date. "People were so enamored of *The Codex* that they would get upset when we didn't post it when we said we were," Malone says. "It was a compliment."

Then Luther got sick, and the Winns moved to a new house. Winn finished putting everything back together in his new bedroom only to have his computer crash. They had backed up the files of the nine completed episodes, but the footage for Episode 10 was lost. It took them three and a half weeks to remake six minutes of video.

None of them had imagined how much time it would take to produce each episode. All of them except Luther were involved in extracurricular activities. Things like AP exams, college visits, choir performances, softball games, and senior events were getting in the way. As fan response heated up, they were fielding lots of personal questions. Finally, after a curious fan outed them by tracing the screen name "Nerrolken" to Winn, they decided to post their bios.

They were getting hits from all over the world and could see that they even had fans at NASA and Apple Computer. On a visit to a university to interview for a scholarship, Foster talked to guys from Virginia Military Institute. One recognized her name, and they told her they loved *The Codex*. People would recognize Malone as the Praetor when they heard his voice.

But by the start of summer, it looked like their ambitious plan to finish the 109-minute movie, Episodes 1 through 20, before leaving for college was doomed.

Winn, Luther, and Malone walked into the A-KON anime and video convention, held every June in Dallas, wearing their *Codex* T-shirts, not knowing what to expect. "I consider myself a dork," Malone says, "but there were a lot of nerds."

They headed for the *Red vs. Blue* table, hoping to meet their heroes: Gus Sorola, "Burnie" Burns, Geoff Ramsey, Kathleen Zuelch, and the rest of the Rooster Teeth crew. "As we were walking up," Malone says, "Gus jumps up and says, 'Are you the guys from *The Codex Series*? Can I take your picture?'"

The teenagers were floored, even more so when the *Red vs. Blue* gang invited them to an after-party. They knocked on room 666 (no kidding) at the Radisson but couldn't enter the party because they weren't twenty-one. Finally, the *Red vs. Blue* crew came out; since the *Codex* kids couldn't go to the party, they all sat in the stairwell and talked shop for forty-five minutes. Way cool.

That summer, *The Codex* took over their lives. The teens virtually camped out at the Winns' house. Winn and Luther played with the game, trying to find new angles for shots. The voice actors worked on different accents for new characters. Except for Winn, they rarely saw their parents.

They stocked up on Goldfish crackers and Bawls, a super-caffeinated drink they bought at a computer store. Becky Winn made them real food like meat loaf, but they mainly consumed enormous amounts of pizza and Blue Bell double-chocolate ice cream. "They called it a download," says Becky Winn. Her grocery bill tripled as teenagers squatted in Alex's bedroom for twelve to eighteen hours a day.

"I was a stress case that whole last month," Malone says. "I hadn't gotten anything done for school. But we really wanted to finish it."

Each night, when everyone finally went home, Winn spent more hours editing, dubbing in the audio, and composing the score. By August, he began to doubt that their project would get finished. "He was so tired, he could hardly even think clearly," Becky Winn says.

Thirty-six hours before Alex was supposed to leave for USC, Luther uploaded Episode 20: "The End of All Things." To date, they have had more than fifteen million visits to their Web site.

Becky Winn remembers Alex lying on the floor when it was done. "I'm exhausted," he told his mother. "Getting to college will feel like a vacation." She thought he was upset, but he was elated. "I love it so much," he told the ceiling. "I know I really want to be a filmmaker."

The Codex Series is now over. Or is it just beginning? In November, the group reunited in Los Angeles to shoot a segment on machinima for mtvU. "It was fricking awesome," Winn says.

Only Malone still bothers to play *Halo*.

An award-winning investigative reporter, **Glenna Whitley** specializes in writing about crime and the legal system. A staff writer for the *Dallas Observer* since November 2003, she's been executive editor and senior writer for *D Magazine* and a feature writer for the *Dallas Morning News*. Whitley's freelance work has appeared in numerous magazines and newspapers, including *Texas Monthly*, *Penthouse*, *Glamour*, *Redbook*, *Ladies Home Journal*, *More*, *New York Times*, *Town & Country*, and many more.

She is co-author with B. G. Burkett of the acclaimed non-fiction book *Stolen Valor* about the Vietnam War, published in 1998. The subject of three segments for TV newsmagazine *20/20*, including one that won a CINE Award, *Stolen Valor* received the 2000 William E. Colby Award for writing on military affairs at Norwich University. The subject of hundreds of stories in magazines and newspapers, *Stolen Valor* is now in development as a TV series.

Her story *Crazy White Mother*, published in the *Dallas Observer*, received the prestigious Texas Headliner's Award for investigative journalism in 2003, her third such award. The judges said: "This is a remarkable example of hard-digging reporting on an elusive subject, delivered in a fast-moving narrative form that tells an amazing tale with color and clarity." In addition, *Crazy White Mother* was a finalist for the 2003 Eugene S. Pulliam National Journalism Writing Award.

Whitley's story *Evil Eyes*, the saga of serial killer Coral Eugene Watts published in June 2003 by the *Dallas Observer*, was featured in an anthology of the best writing from alternative newspapers published by Penguin in 2005. Another story was included in *D Magazine's Dallas: The 30 Greatest Stories Ever Told*, published September 2004. Whitley has received numerous awards for investigative reporting on criminal affairs from the Texas Bar Association, the Dallas Bar Association, the Dallas Press Club, and the City and Regional Magazine Association.

A graduate of Texas A&M University, Whitley lives in Dallas with her husband Peter and two sons, Eric and Andrew.

Charlie W. Starr

BROKEN HALOS

Science, Religion, and Ethics in Halo

Does God exist in the Halo *universe? If so, which side is He on?*

SCIENCE FICTION WAS BORN OF RELIGION. Stop! Don't flip to the next essay...let me explain.

There's a reason we love fantastic stories. It's that we want fantastic experiences. We want them so much that we'll take them in as many ways as we can get—through our own experiences, through stories of other peoples' lives, even through experiences we invent. This desire for the fantastic finds constant connection to those impulses we term *religious*. Sometimes the connections are obvious, and sometimes they're convoluted, but they're deeply woven throughout the very fibers of the *Halo*verse.

Consider, for example, the story of Dr. Halsey, a character insignificant in the Halo games but important in the books. Her subplot deals with the question of ethics in science. From the outset, she questions the morality of using mechanical technology, bioengineering, and behavior modification to transform a group of children into advanced killing machines christened the SPARTAN-IIs. She has to purposely withdraw from the children emotionally, refusing to call them by name and, instead, referring to them as "test subjects" (*The Fall of Reach* 26, 30–31).

In addition to taking them away from their parents, Dr. Halsey turns the children into warriors, then into enhanced superhumans, a process that leaves half of them dead or deformed (60–62). At one point in the story, even Cortana wonders, "Was Dr. Halsey a monster? Or just doing what had to be done to protect humanity? Perhaps a little of both" (270). Halsey attempts to play the odds, pretend to be scientifically objective (i.e., act without human heart), and assume the Frankensteinian role of man playing God. *Frankenstein* was subtitled *The Modern Prometheus*, and it's from there that we gather the connection between "hard science" SF and the religious impulse.

Prometheus, the only god among the Titans to side with Zeus and the Olympians, gave mankind fire—that's the part of the story that everyone knows. What many don't know is that Prometheus also gave humanity *techné*, the practical arts. Techné, or technology, became the divine gift that offered the means for us to make our lives matter. In technology we find our Godhood, and we also run into the limitations of our humanity.

But technology without humanity cannot save us. Something divine calls us to draw limits to our attempts to replace God with ourselves, and the results of such God-play through techné are always the same: Faustus loses his soul to the devil, Frankenstein creates a monster, and, in a sadly prophetic example of life imitating art, Oppenheimer creates the A-bomb, proclaiming humanity's horrid self deification when he quotes from the Hindu myth: "I am become Death, the destroyer of worlds." Technology makes the Borg (like Darth Vader) "more machine than man," and the Forerunners create the Halos to contain the Flood. Their reward for this grand, almost divine achievement is their own extinction. Dr. Halsey finds the limits of technology in her recognition that she should have been concerned with compassion, love, and saving lives (*First Strike* 245) rather than rising above such apparent human frailties.

Science fiction and science itself are inextricably intertwined with our religious impulses. The connection between our own divine spark and our pursuit of technology links back, beyond the rise of science at the height of an utterly Christian Europe,[1] to the earliest stories of hu-

---

[1] Granted the trouble Galileo had with the church, it is nevertheless a common misconception that science and religion have always been at odds. Philosopher Alfred North Whitehead notes that apart from Christianity's "insistence on the rationality of God," science would not have developed. The first scientists of the thirteenth century were driven by a belief in an orderly universe built by an orderly God. Only in the eighteenth century when philosophical materialism intruded itself into scientific empiricism were faith and science put at odds.

man creation and achievement. There is an experience for which we hunger—have hungered for since the beginning of humanity. We use words for it like *awe, wonder, mystery,* or *romanticism.* We call it a desire for *transcendence,* the wholly *Other,* the *Divine—God.*

So-called *realistic* stories are new to human history—only a few hundred years old. The earliest human stories were the great myths of which we remain aware today, tales of divine experience and human encounters with gods. There were no other stories worth telling. These were followed in the Medieval West by epic romances. God receded from the story as a character, but the hero of ancient myth remained, evolving into the knight in search of a grail that would draw him closer to divine worlds, magical dimensions.

With the Age of Reason and the rise of scientific materialism, fantastic stories became unreasonable, the "fantastic" only "fantasy" (that is, the opposite of fact), and transcendent myth nothing but false mythology. Fiery Helios was knocked out of his sun-chariot and cast from his journey across the sky when science stripped magic from the world and told us that the sun was nothing but a big ball of gas. The problem: we still demanded sunsets be beautiful. We still demanded experiences of wonder, awe, and mystery.

Transcendent Stories in the Age of Fact

Fantastic stories went in two directions at this time. One was fantasy;[2] the other, science fiction, began with writers like Jules Verne and H. G. Wells. As science removed one kind of mystery and wonder from the Earth, the human soul nevertheless continued to demand mystery, wonder, and transcendence.[3] The place of mystery, no longer the magic wood or sacred mount, became space, the ocean bottom, the moon, Mars, and other planets. Angels became aliens, magic turned into advanced technology, dragons became dinosaurs, awe became evolutionary transcendence, God became an extraterrestrial panspermia,[4] and salvation became the product of our own technological advancement.

---

[2] Fantasy, in my mind, only survived the twentieth century onslaught of Modernism thanks to the "sub-created" realism (in an age when we demanded everything be "realistic") that was brought to it by J. R. R. Tolkien in The Lord of the Rings.

[3] See *2001: A Space Odyssey.*

[4] Again, *2001.*

Our warrior heroes became scientists, their chariots submarines and spaceships, their magic swords ray guns.

Our longings for wonder, mystery, transcendence, Divinity—our deep spiritual longings, our religious impulses—are the hungers that drive science fiction stories, stories that satisfy our hunger for magic and mystery in an age that has denied magic and claimed the ability to solve all mysteries.

It is for this same reason that two primary branches of science fiction exist today. The first continues the vision of H. G. Wells, Arthur C. Clarke, and Isaac Asimov.[5] The second is represented by such writers as Frank Herbert, Orson Scott Card, and filmmaker George Lucas.[6] The well-known distinction of "hard science SF" from "science fantasy" is close to what I'm suggesting here, but doesn't quite capture it. Instead, I'm talking about a difference between a kind of SF that demythifies the cosmos and one that remythifies it. In this second category, which certainly can include an emphasis on hard science and technology, *Supernature* cannot be necessarily explained or reduced, religious impulses aren't dismissed, and technology isn't as important a solution to problems as is the human heart.

My main point so far is simply this: that even the SF that demythifies acknowledges by its very existence our refusal to let our religious impulses go. Wonder, mystery, and transcendence *will* be satisfied. Thus we enter the *Halo*verse, a place where we find our religious impulses existing paradoxically in a world where religion otherwise doesn't belong.

Halo's Double Vision: The Negative

Religion in *Halo* is treated like Bantha Fodder. My own personal *Halo* sensei, Daniel Lewis, sees the Covenant prophets as "space popes" govern-

---

[5] This approach emphasizes humanism—where mankind is his own end, his goodness a matter of evolutionary progress past his *primitive* need for religion (the last book in Clarke's Odyssey series, *3001*, contains a great example—those with religious impulses in this future are considered insane), and which holds to a Naturalism in which all wondrous, magical things still have a *scientific* (which is to say purely natural, utterly knowable) explanation, even if that explanation is of a highly advanced technology we can't yet understand or of a highly evolved alien species capable of God-like powers we may one day attain.

[6] Lucas, of course, being the least concerned with the science of his SF and more with the mythic story it tells.

ing a militant "space Islam." Religious language, that is, the language of the Covenant, is replete with the stereotypical language (their polytheism aside) of terrorist Jihadists. When we first meet the Covenant in *Reach*, their initial communiqué to humanity is, "Your destruction is the will of the Gods...and we are their instruments" (98). In *The Flood*, Zuka Zamamee inspires his troops with promises of glorious death: "The Prophets have blessed this mission, have blessed *you*, and want every soldier to know that those who transcend the physical will be welcomed into paradise" (210). In *First Strike*, fanaticism is apparent; the Covenant AI constantly screams "Infidel" at Cortana (170), and Cortana monitors the Covenant's "excited religious babble:...*uncovering the fragment of divinity and illuminating shard of the gods*" (192–93) and "*Minor artifacts discovered; rejoice!*" (197). In *Halo 2*, anyone who fails the Covenant has broken the covenant and is therefore a heretic, as is anyone who challenges the truth of the Prophets, like the Heretic who claims the Prophets are false and leading the people of the Covenant to the ruin.

The Arbiter sent to kill this Heretic is the Elite who failed to keep Halo from destruction. The harshness of Covenant religion is revealed in his punishment: "Soon the Great Journey shall begin. But when it does, the weight of your heresy will stay your feet, and you shall be left behind" (*Halo 2*). Other cheesy religious lines include the Covenant being on a "march to glorious salvation," and the Prophet of Regret's mantra about activating the second Halo ring (when we know by then that his beliefs are agonizingly wrong): "I shall light this holy ring, release its cleansing flame, and burn a path into the divine beyond" (*Halo 2*).

But what really suggests that the *Halo*verse has it in for religion is the introductory chapter of *The Flood*, where we meet Covenant characters for the first time—their characterization is laughably that of radical-fundamentalist superiority and hostility. When Ship Master Orna 'Fulsamee speaks for the first time, he snidely refers to humans as "filthy primates [who] somehow merited an actual name" (4) and "filthy creatures" speaking a "barbaric tongue" (5). Even more telling is the Covenant's attitude toward each other: 'Fulsamee compares the Prophet species to "tiny, squealing rodents he had hunted in his childhood" (5), is angered by their use of the "royal 'we'" (6), and is incensed by the Covenant's theology of zealous desire to "transcend the physical." The (majority of the) Covenant are hateful, angry, judgmental beings in love with death. We are meant to despise them and their religion (*Halo*).

The Prophets are authoritarian, the Elites are sycophantic, and Tartarus and his Brutes...well...savage brutes. We come to like one of them, the Arbiter, a little bit, but only as he comes to understand that his religion is false. I take that back; there's another character for whom we gain some sympathy, a Grunt named Yayap whom we meet in *The Flood*. All this poor little guy wants to do is survive, but he only adds to our loathing of Covenant religion by emphasizing the inequality of their caste system: "The Prophets had long made use of his race as cannon fodder" (*The Flood* 32). The triumvirate of this hierarchy, the three Prophets of Regret, Truth, and Mercy, don't inspire any love for Covenant religion themselves (*Halo 2*), nor does the in-fighting between Brutes and Elites—the two leading, competing factions of this religion of terror.

Most importantly, though, religion fares poorly in *Halo* when it comes in contact with the demythifying power of Naturalistic explanation. The Covenant religion is proven false throughout the games and books. In the first game, as in the *Flood* novel, it begins when we meet 343 Guilty Spark, that loveable little genocidal robot who begins to demythify the Halo. The cat (or Flood) is let completely out of the bag for us when Cortana explains to the Master Chief how the ring works and why the Forerunners built it:

> Halo doesn't kill Flood—it kills their *food*. Human, Covenant, whatever. You're all equally edible. The only way to stop the Flood is to starve them to death. And that's exactly what Halo is designed to do. Wipe the galaxy clean of *all* sentient life (*The Flood* 256).

The debunking of Covenant religion continues in *Halo 2*. The Covenant thinks 343 Guilty Spark is an Oracle, a label that the floating bot finds annoyingly inaccurate. When the Flood is released, a Prophet announces the finding of a second Halo, promising that its "divine wind will rush through the stars, propelling all who are worthy along the path to salvation" (*Halo 2*). Now that they have the "sacred icon" (the Index), the "Great Journey" will begin and bring salvation to all. But we shortly thereafter learn from Gravemind that 2401 Penitent Tangent's containment and the Prophet of Regret's "Great Journey" are the same. Gravemind continues: "Your Prophets have promised you freedom from a doomed existence, but you will find no salvation on this ring" (*Halo 2*).

The Arbiter eventually comes to believe this truth, telling Tartarus, "There are things about *Halo* even the hierarchs do not understand"

(*Halo 2*). Tartarus calls this "blasphemy," even though he has heard 343 Guilty Spark complete the demythification of Covenant religion. When asked, "What are the rings?", 343 nonchalantly answers, "Weapons of last resort," created by the Forerunners to destroy all "potential Flood hosts," thus halting the spread of the Flood. When all else failed, the Forerunners activated the rings, killing themselves and all other sentient life in the galaxy. The Arbiter pleads: "Tartarus. The Prophets have betrayed us."

There are *some* religious nods in *Halo*, first appearing in the form of technology and names. John is a Demon, Tartarus the head Brute; weapons have names like MJOLNIR armor,[7] Shiva nukes, Scarabs, Shades, Ghosts, Wraiths, and Banshees. Additionally, there are the UNSC AI's otherworldly avatars: a mermaid, a samurai warrior, and "one made entirely of bright light with comets trailing in her wake" (*Reach* 114). But these are only words and appearances, applying mythic allusions to a mythless vision of the religious. At best, this method only connects back to the theme of techné and man's attempt to make himself divine through technology,[8] a God-play that Dr. Halsey learns to reject.

The love of technology is apparent in the books and born of the game's feature of offering great variety in weaponry.[9] In *The Flood*, Captain Keyes offers this hope: the fact that the Covenant does not make new technology but scavenges among other cultures for it "may prove to be their undoing" (132). By the end of *Halo*, of course, we know that the Covenant's scavenging of "holy relics" or "useful technology" (*The Flood* 270) leads to the release of the Flood and the possible extinction of all races in the galaxy. More ominous is the creature Gravemind's self definition to John—"I am a monument to all *your* sins" (*Halo 2*—emphasis added)—suggesting that the Flood may have been produced by human technology.[10]

Technology is thus both the divine hope and annihilation of humanity. Dr. Halsey understands the dilemma. To save humanity she has had to act inhumanely toward a group of children, turning them into gods of

---

[7] Which makes the Spartans look like "Greek war gods" (*Reach* 1).

[8] Or even better than divine—the Spartans are described as "far more effective and ruthless than Homer's gods had ever been" (*Reach* 1).

[9] Which proves to be tedious in the books—check out page eighty in *Reach*; the entire page is nothing but a list of weapons and technology!

[10] Which is to say, by Forerunner technology, if hints that humanity descended from the Forerunners are revealed to be true in *Halo 3*.

"machine and nerve" (*Halo 2*). Says Halsey, "that's what the SPARTAN-II project was all about, wasn't it? Playing God for the greater good" (*First Strike* 124). Eventually, Halsey comes to the realization that this was a mistake. This is her final lesson to John:

> For a long time I had thought that we had to sacrifice a few for the good of the entire human race....I have killed and maimed and caused a great deal of suffering to many people—all in the name of self preservation....But now I'm not sure that philosophy has worked out too well. I should have been trying to save every single human life—no matter what it cost (245).

It is this new understanding that technology makes us gods only by destroying our humanity that Dr. Halsey puts into action at the end of *First Strike*, first in giving the Forerunner gravity crystal to Locklear to destroy (274–75, 284), and second in explaining to John the choice that lay in his hands regarding saving Sgt. Johnson from death at the hands of the ONI through objective, scientific experimentation (245–47). John struggles with the moral dilemma, finally deciding Sgt. Johnson's life matters more than the technological advancement his death might produce (335–36).

Admiral Whitcomb shows his understanding of this dilemma in a sincere and overtly religious moment in *Halo*. Realizing that he is about to sacrifice hundreds of sailors to save Earth, he nevertheless laments: "Hundreds for billions....Duty be damned...I'm still going to burn in hell for this....Go, Cortana. Get us out of here. And God forgive me" (282). In the end, however, religion as it appears plainly in *Halo* receives a consistently negative treatment, either by making it, at worst, the source of all evil, and, at best, ancillary and flat.

Halo's Double Vision: The Positive

But it's not all atheism and negativity in the *Haloverse*. Overt religion may take its hits, but religious sensibility exists in subtler forms in *Halo*; humanity cannot break itself of the hunger for divine encounter. This appears in its most subtle form as the presence of religious metaphors in *Halo*.

The Spartans are a metaphor for divine presence in terms of their stature, battle prowess, and, especially, in their role as heroic inspirations to other soldiers. All who look at them do so with awe. *Halo 2* begins with an award ceremony celebrating the Master Chief's recent successes in battle. John would have none of it, but Sgt. Johnson reminds him that "[f]olks need heroes."

The ancient and as yet mysterious Forerunners come across with the same quality of indifference and distance that we find among the gods of Greek tragedy. Cortana, conversely, makes an apt metaphor for the general idea in religion of the Divine Presence coming into an oracle and the specifically Christian vision of the indwelling of the Holy Spirit of God. She is the voice who enters John's armor to speak truth and provide guidance through his world. And she is the Sanctifying[11] Spirit that helps him "utilize the suit[12] more effectively" (*Reach* 236, 252).

The *Halo*verse also has its own hell, and the Flood are its demons. They hunger for sentient souls, possessing bodies and minds, as is gruesomely described in the possession of Captain Keyes: "As Keyes began to lose touch with the rest of his body, something foul entered it...polluting his brain with a hunger so base that it would have made him vomit, had he any possession of his own body" (*The Flood* 175). The Flood forms take normal bodies and turn them into grotesque versions of their former selves: "The alien's skull was canted at a sickening angle, as if the bones of its neck had been softened or liquefied. It hung limply down the creature's back, lifeless—like a limb that needed amputation" (*The Flood* 223). The Master Chief enters this hellish world beneath Halo's surface without the divine presence of Cortana, who remains in the ring library (*Halo*). There he finds the helmet of a marine named Jenkins and replays a video massacre. As for Jenkins, who is possessed but remains partially aware, "[s]omehow, without actually dying, he had been sentenced to hell" (*The Flood* 276).

Halo 2 presents the metaphor of a Christ figure in the unlikely person of the Arbiter. He is unjustly accused of heresy, hung by his arms in a fashion that resembles Christ on the cross (he's even standing on a cross in the cut clip), tortured to symbolic death, resurrected as the Arbiter, and given assignments intended to lead to his death as a scapegoat for the high council.[13] He fights against the religious leaders of his day and saves

---

[11] *Sanctification* is the Christian idea of supernatural transformation by God of the human psyche into a spiritual type of Himself. See the New Testament book of Romans, especially chapters seven and eight.

[12] See Romans 13:12.

[13] The New Testament book of Hebrews speaks of Christ as the arbiter (high priest) between mankind and God.

all sentient life when he stops the firing of the ring. Finally, there is the apocalyptic threat of the firing of the Halos. Even as 343 Guilty Spark demythifies the Covenant religion, revealing the horrible truth, the gamer experiences the magnitude of this revelation: Armageddon is at hand.

Thus, while religion is consciously marginalized in *Halo*, religious symbolism pervades the story, contributing to the ritual experience of mystery and magic that the game creates for its players. But that isn't all. The hunger for wonder and awe inherent in all of us is present beyond symbols in the game. It's present in the very nature of *the game itself*.

To play the game is to *experience* wonder and awe. The act of taking the journey as a first-person shooter is what creates the experience—that, combined with a filmic quality to the graphics (especially the cut clips), pulls us into the *Halo*verse, making us characters in the movie. As *Halo* opens, Gregorian chants over filmic images draw us in with graphics and sounds that the Xbox was able to bring to new levels for gamers. I find particularly effective the use of this music early in *Halo 2*, when the Master Chief floats through slow motion space to deliver a Covenant bomb from Mac platform Cairo to an enemy ship. He's like an avenging angel, descending from the serenity of heaven to wreak destruction on Sodom.

The best games are immersive in this way: not appealing to left-brained intellect, but right-brained imagination, the faculty in us that makes wonder possible. Immersive games have the same kind of mythic appeal we experience when entering Tolkien's Middle Earth. It is to enter a complete world, what Tolkien called a "sub-creation" ("On Fairy Stories" 60), a world that is consistent and complete and has already been going on for thousands of years.

We get this depth of age in the *Halo*verse through such elements as the finding of ancient Forerunner artifacts and allusions to the past like the "taming of the Hunters" and the "Grunt Rebellion" (*Halo 2*). It's true that *Halo* is, at times, its own worst enemy in this regard, throwing in Grunts that sound like Jawas, pop-culture audio bytes like "cheeky monkey" (*Halo 2*), and silly phrases in the bottom right corner of the display, all of which serve to add a campiness to the *Halo*verse that identifies its unreal-estate. These drawbacks, however, are minor; they add some humor, and the sub-created experience of wonder remains powerful.

In addition to fulfilling our hunger for wonder, awe, and transcendent experience, *Halo* also fulfills our desire for mystery. To play the game is to experience one mystery after another. Even though these mysteries get explained as the player progresses, these explanations come only after hard-fought experience, like divine revelations of untold things. And with every mystery solved, new and deeper mysteries arise, satisfying our continual need for wonder.

The first mystery we encounter in *Halo* is the game itself. Every new level requires hours of familiarizing oneself with new topography and architecture and with discerning what tactics will bring victory—all of this while being constantly shot at. The rewards for solving these mysteries are plot advancement (in each new cut clip) and new mysteries at every turn.[14] Each new struggle finds new levels (literally) of revelation and, as such, a struggle to enlightenment, like the discipline of virtual monks following their intricate eye/hand mantras to Nirvana, a game controller replacing prayer beads.

Think back to your initial encounter with *Halo* for another great example of experiential mystery. It's your first time through the story, so you've maybe been playing for five or six hours. You know who the enemy is, you know who you have to face—more Covenant. Suddenly you start seeing dead aliens everywhere. Something's not right. Then you hear fragments of marine com, hysterical fear in the voices. You find a helmet belonging to a guy named Jenkins, and from his point of view watch in filmic flashback the rise of a new enemy even deadlier and more horrifying than the Covenant. Suspense is high till the mystery is revealed, and you finally face the Flood yourself. Then mystery quickly follows mystery in the form of rapid-fire plot twists: 343 Guilty Spark, who seems to know you ("Reclaimer") and is happy to see you, followed by Cortana's revelation that Guilty Spark and his laser drones are yet another new enemy and you have to destroy Halo or humanity is doomed.

Then, in *Halo 2*, you are John the Spartan, sinking into a lake when suddenly a booming, venomous voice says, "This is not your grave, but you are welcome in it," and tendrils reach up and gently take hold of your body. We meet the God-like Gravemind, whose origins are shrouded in darkling hints. It speaks in rhyme, its revelations convoluted and half-true. The Arbiter calls it a "parasite," offering the first hint of its

---

[14] See *The Flood*, page 93, for a really nice example of this. Cortana learns the true purpose of the rings but refuses to tell John, saying there's no time to explain. He only learns the truth after facing the Flood and retrieving the Index.

connection to the Flood. Even as it demythifies the Covenant religion, it adds mystery by what it reveals and by its very presence.

The books have their own share of mysteries to add to the *Halo*verse. These include the mysterious space/time warping crystal in *First Strike*, Dr. Halsey's secret plan with Kelly (*First Strike* 334), and, most especially, the fact that John and the other Spartans find the Forerunner language to be strangely familiar,[15] having the appearance of Aztec symbols to John (*Reach* 223) and Greek writing to Fred (*First Strike* 142). This familiarity, along with John's ability to operate the Halo controls instinctively, in a way that "almost seemed hard-wired, like his fight-or-flight response" (*Flood* 170), brings us to the *Halo*verse's greatest mystery of all: Who were the Forerunners? Ample clues are given throughout the games and books, clues that most Halophiles have probably already linked together and to which *Halo 3* will hopefully provide answers. I have my theory, but here I'm not as interested in answers as I am in the experience of transcendent mystery that questions and clues provide.

Halo is an experience of gaming that plays to the very religious impulses its overt treatment of religion decries. It is in the first-person (shooter) confrontation with mystery and with dark and ancient forces other than ourselves that *Halo* achieves what science tried to eliminate and SF tried to satisfy. But it *can't* be eliminated. It can be satisfied only for a time.

The Timeless Wish

Still, *Halo* leaves us in paradox. The *Halo*verse is one that satisfies the hunger for mythic encounters but demythifies the Divine, reducing it to the merely material. It raises humanity to Godhood but denies Godhood to humanity (in fact, it punishes their hubris). *Halo* proves (even as it tries to deny) that our spiritual longings can't be set aside. To end there, however, would be sad. This game, and others, may satisfy those longings for a time, but, in the end, the hunger returns. Hopefully, the first-person (and increasingly filmic) game hails what I think the waning of Realism does:[16] if the twentieth century was an experiment in

---

[15] See *Reach* 270, *Flood* 170, and *First Strike* 113, 238.

[16] As does the increase in popular appreciation for films that are epic in scope and fantastic in content.

finding man's place in a world without God, the twenty-first century will hopefully be an experiment in finding God's place in man's world.

But even that wouldn't be enough. The thesis I've been weaving throughout the content of this essay is simple: *hunger* proves the existence of *food*. Our own hunger, then—here in the Natureverse—for transcendent experiences, for wonder, awe, mystery, Divinity, and immortality, is proof of the existence of such food in the transcendent, wondrous, awe-inspiring, mysterious, Divine, and immortal verse of Supernature to which ours is attached. Our religious impulses, these hungers for food unseen, which many of us nevertheless have tasted in experience, are not mere ignorant, unscientific stupidity. Perhaps we are returning to this realization in the twenty-first century. Perhaps we'll even take it farther, achieving more than just finding the place of God in *our* world. Perhaps we'll eventually come to understand *our* place in *His*.

Charlie W. Starr teaches English, humanities, and film at Kentucky Christian University in Eastern Kentucky, where he also makes movies with his students and family. He writes articles, teaches Sunday school, and has published three books: one on Romans, the second an SF novel called *The Heart of Light*, and his third book, *Honest to God*, was released by Navpress in the summer of 2005. This anthology is the sixth Charlie has contributed to for BenBella Books. He enjoys writing, reading classic literature, watching bad television, and movies of every kind. His areas of expertise as a teacher include literature, film, and all things C. S. Lewis. Charlie describes his wife Becky as "a full of life, full-blood Cajun who can cook like one, too." They have two children: Bryan, who wants to be the next Steven Spielberg, and Alli, who plays a pretty mean piano. You can find more on Charlie's books and look at some of the movies he's made at his Web site: http://campus.kcu.edu/faculty/cstarr.

REFERENCES

Dietz, William C. *Halo: The Flood*. New York: Ballantine Books, 2003.

Nylund, Eric. *Halo: The Fall of Reach*. New York: Del Rey Books, 2001.

——. *Halo: First Strike*. New York: Ballantine Books, 2003.

Olasky, Marvin. "Spreading Salt." Interview with Scholar Alvin J. Schmidt. *World Magazine*. 16 April 2005.

Tolkien, J. R. R. "On Fairy-Stories." *Essays Presented to Charles Williams*. Ed. C. S. Lewis. Grand Rapids: William B. Eerdmans, 1968. 38–89.

Whitehead, Alfred North. Quoted by Alvin J. Schmidt. See Olasky.

Halo: Combat Evolved. Bungie Studios. Microsoft Game Studios. 15 Nov 2001. Xbox.

Halo 2. Bungie Studios. Microsoft Game Studios. 9 Nov 2004. Xbox.

Jill MacKay

THE MODERN MYTHOS

A brief guide to the hidden secrets of Halo.

HALO: COMBAT EVOLVED was released in 2001, often shipped out with Microsoft's new console, the Xbox, as part of a package. Pitting the player against boldly colored aliens on a colossal ring world, it does not appear to be an intellectually stimulating game of choice for players around the globe. With dialogue directly lifted from *Aliens* (1986) and names plucked from previous Bungie games, one could attribute *Halo's* references to the mishmash of pop culture that surrounds us, the MTV generation's legacy. As one of the editors in charge of the "Story and Speculations Page" on *Halo's* largest fan site, I am privy to deep thoughts, idle dreamings, and rampant speculation from all walks of life, concerning every conceivable aspect of the Halo games. Allow me, in seven easy steps, to lead you through a brief summary of the complicated origins that comprise the very modern mythology that surrounds *Halo*.

Septology

Most of the *Halo* fans who are interested in the story surrounding the Master Chief's journey start with one assumption: a spade is never a mere spade, and over-analyzing is impossible. It was not that I found seven obvious points about which to talk, or that seven was the first number to spring to mind. In *Halo*, seven has a special significance. Drawing from history, religion, and other cultural references—seven rings to rule them all—the number seven pops up in the *Halo* universe with surprising frequency. For the uneducated or the newcomer, one may see it first in the form of his or her avatar. The Master Chief's designation is 117, and the odd player might think that it seems familiar. He or she might link the Chief's name, John, to a book of the Bible and equate 117 to chapter one, verse seventeen, if he or she is so inclined. Incidentally, in the Book of Revelation, the Revelation of Saint John the Divine say:

> And when I saw him, I fell at his feet as dead. And he laid his right hand upon me, saying unto me, Fear not; I am the first and the last.[1]

Most are likely to dismiss this as the result of an unimaginative writer picking a few connected tidbits in an attempt to add a much-needed air of mysticism to an otherwise simple space story. The next, most obvious reference to the number seven would be the level (and character) titled "343 Guilty Spark." Those grounded in Bungie lore might realize that the number three is used when a significant plot point is being signaled, and that 343 is the result of seven times seven times seven. Here, another Bible reference is made when the dreaded Flood is released to cleanse the universe, one that is undoubtedly familiar to all those who have read the story of Noah and his Ark. As the player is drawn into the *Halo* world, the tally of sevens begins to grow. In the sequel, we see characters named 2401 Penitent Tangent, seven Halos represented in a hologram, and poems with rhyming couplets in sevens. It's even been speculated that some weapons work best when seven shots are fired. Search deeper, and you'll find that the official timeline sees the government formed in 2170; that the character of the AI, Cortana, has a lifespan of seven years; and that time anomalies are resolved on September 7, 2552. It would be more difficult to search for consistent references to numbers other than the mythical seven. Incidentally, from Earth you can only see seven natural celestial bodies.

---

[1] The Holy Bible, New International Version, Hodder and Stoughton 1985, p. 1234.

Marathon

The number seven extends beyond the *Halo* universe, being featured in Bungie's own history. The games that preceded *Halo* are all shown due respect by means of sly, and not-so-sly, references in the Halo games themselves. While *ONI* and *Myth* both receive a doff of the cap, it is the Marathon series that is the true predecessor. Like *Halo*, *Marathon* is a story of man against aliens, fighting seemingly impossible odds.[2] To understand the link between the games, one must look at the themes running through them both. They concern highly advanced races that are now all but gone from the universe. These races were the Jjaro and Forerunners from *Marathon* and *Halo*, respectively. The traces of their civilizations can be seen in the artifacts they have left behind, and the Forerunner have left something more, something deadly. The dreaded Flood released in *Halo* was known to the Forerunners, and they seemed intent upon studying it. Despite the danger, the Forerunner kept specimens alive for study. Remnants of the Forerunner civilization, such as 343 Guilty Spark, even express an apparent appreciation that some form of the Flood has survived. Likewise, the Jjaro had contained a dangerous creature of chaos, W'rckcacnter, within a sun, but had not destroyed it. The Jjaro believed it would be imprisoned for all time. The Forerunner also seemed to possess the technology to contain the Flood, at least to a certain extent. The use of this technology is highly sought after now they have been released, though its cure is morally ambiguous. In *Halo*, to rid the galaxy of the virulent Flood, the galaxy must be made devoid of all sentient life. However drastic this seems, the alternative is that the Flood overruns the star systems. The Forerunner seemed to think the trade-off was worth it, as we know the Halos were activated once. It is worth noting that the Master Chief aims to disable the Halos to stop this annihilation, choosing instead to attempt to fight the Flood through more conventional means. He is hampered by the Covenant, a collection of alien races who revere the Forerunners as gods. They believe that the firing of the Halo installations will speed them on the path to enlightenment. The Jjaro suffered a similar degradation at the hands of the Pfhor, who used the technology left scattered around the universe. The

---

[2] Strangely enough, for a predecessor, *Marathon* is actually set in a future time frame to *Halo*. Some gamers who have played and studied both noted that *Marathon* had a conspicuous gap in its timeline where *Halo* could slot in nicely, but this theory has been discredited by Bungie.

exact natures of the Forerunner's and Jjaro's departures from the universe are never fully explained, nor are the years of lost history.

Legends

Bungie does not draw purely on its own past for inspiration; throughout the Halo series we are inundated with references to great fables from our own history. The Greek legends are the most obvious. John-117, our eyes and ears in the *Halo* universe, is apparently the last member of the SPARTAN-II program: a series of super soldiers augmented with cybernetic implants and trained from a very early age in the craft of war. So far, so like the Spartans of old (sans technology, of course). In ancient Sparta, the individual was trained to become a warrior and his needs set aside, less important than the need to protect Greece. Again, this seems like an obvious similarity, but the more dedicated gamer has searched further: drawn parallels with the Spartans' defeat at Thermopylae (a name brought up in *Marathon*) and found even a Persian army in the *Halo* universe. The Covenant, as the enemy, can easily be seen as the Persians. Also, the Spartan hero, Dienekes, is the same age as John-117. The truly interesting point comes when one talks about the army of Ten Thousand Immortals. In the *Halo* universe, we have an army of immortal foes, the Flood. Worryingly, it is the battle of Thermopylae that came to be the Spartans last stand. For all of these neat little connections, some of these theories do not hold water. The Persians were allied with the Ten Thousand Immortals, whereas the Covenant and the Flood are as much enemies as humanity is with both. The Persians were also a unified force, whereas, in *Halo 2*, we learn that the Covenant is in fact a fractioning group, with a civil war threatening. Still, for the references to come so fast and thick, it seems odd that Bungie would choose the Spartan name without intending to link it to some factor of the past. Could the Covenant, in fact, be a representation of the Greeks, betrayed by their own? Looking away from Greek mythology, the Norse gods are also paid their due by Bungie, again by means of the avatar, John. The armor worn by John-117 is designated mjolnir, the hammer of Thor. The symbol is associated with unstoppable strength, but also regeneration. As the last of his kind and humanity's last hope in a desperate war against the Flood, the MJOLNIR battle suit is as much an icon of hope as it is of strength and violence.

Culture

With ancient history behind us, Bungie readily pays tribute to humanity's more recent past by paying particular attention to the best science fiction literature around. The concept of a Ringworld will not be unknown to fans of Larry Niven and Ian M. Banks; even *Star Trek* featured a Dyson Sphere. As Bungie seems to make a habit of burying information in plain sight, it would make sense for these references to have some sort of parallel in the *Halo* universe. One has to scrabble to find more than the most obvious link. If crawling through claustrophobic corridors to find overlarge, violent, and merciless aliens reminds the player of *Aliens*, it is not a huge surprise. It must be understood that Bungie did not set out to create a television series, film, or a novel. Video games, by their very nature, require a huge effort on the part of the creator, and story design often comes second, third, and fourth to more important pursuits, such as user interfaces, in-game physics, and lines of code. Despite attempts to link the mysterious Forerunner to the mysterious aliens of whichever science fiction parable you choose, it is tempting to say, simply, that Bungie uses these references as a hook. When the player is comforted by the recognizable, he or she is less likely to put the game down.

Sword

Despite this rare blip in the almost pathological disregard for mere coincidences, there may be other Bungie "clues" that, upon closer inspection, turn out to be only happenstance. Foe Hammer, the trusty drop pilot in *Halo*, shares a name with another pop culture reference. *Lord of the Rings* fans will know that Gandalf's sword, Glamdring, literally translates to *foe hammer*. Familiarity breeds complacency; perhaps Bungie is only throwing out a few red herrings, and this appears to be the case until one looks closer. The other female character in *Halo*, Cortana the AI, is also named for a sword. Her name is a distortion of *curtana*, a short sword that has had its tip removed. Edward the Confessor used his curtana as the Sword of Mercy—a comforting thought that the Master Chief's greatest ally is named for such virtue. As her character is one upon whom the Master Chief and the other human forces depend, she is certainly a worthy bearer of the name. Her compassion for the lost human forces is what grounds the player in the game and, hopefully, spurs him onward in his quest. Curiously, another sword named Cortana, the sword of Ogier the Dane, bore an inscription, as well. This inscription mentions Durendal, a variant of the name Durandal, the treacherous AI in the Marathon series. Yet again, this seems to be another soft reference to *Halo*'s spiritual predecessor, until one learns more of Cortana's inscription. This says, "[I] am of the same steel and temper as Joyeuse and Durendal." Suddenly, our thoughts are not so comforting when we realize that the Master Chief gives control of the galaxy's super weapon entirely over to Cortana, *against* the advice of the Forerunner monitor. Cortana's motives have been widely debated, but there is no arguing that the name is hinting at something. In the trailer for *Halo 3*, she bluntly states, "I am your shield, I am your sword." Just as the original Curtana was broken by an intervening angel in order to stop a wrongful killing, perhaps the other characters in *Halo* warrant a closer inspection. The self-proclaimed monument to all our sins is the Flood master, Gravemind. He is no angel, at least not by human reckoning. Yet, he is the only character we've seen who appears powerful enough to challenge Cortana, and at the end of *Halo 2* she has no choice but to listen to him.

Rampancy

When one is inspecting the character of Cortana, it is all too easy to find comparisons to the aforementioned Durandal, partly because of their shared sword heritage as swords, but also because both are powerful artificial intelligences. Durandal's betrayal of his crew was instigated by his growing rampancy. Rampancy is Bungie's answer to Asimov's laws. Created by one of Bungie's writers, the term describes the four stages of development that an AI undergoes when it has absorbed too much information. Rampancy can be seen as true self awareness, evolution, or plain insanity on the part of the AI, and, seemingly without fail, it leads to trouble. Bearing in mind that *Marathon*, and therefore Durandal, is only meant to act as a spiritual predecessor to *Halo* and by extension Cortana, the exact nature of Cortana and rampancy is a subject of much debate. In the *Halo* tie-in novel, *The Fall of Reach*, by Eric Nylund, Cortana is labelled as a "smart" AI. She is cloned directly from a human brain and, therefore, has an advantage over her so-called "dumb" peers. Her abilities to learn and think like a human, while coupled with the astounding processing power and knowledge of a computer, make her a valuable tool to the Master Chief. All things come at a price, however, and Cortana's is a short life span. She will live for only seven years before she has gathered too much information for her mind to process; she will literally think herself to death. As Cortana is portrayed as a vivacious and spirited character, it would not be a stretch of the imagination to think that she would be reluctant to die. Her fate may be presumed, but Cortana is possibly not resigned to it. She spends a great deal of time in the Forerunner databanks on the Halo Installation 04 and shows visual changes to her holographic matrix, including flaring red when angry and green when the Master Chief talks to 343 Guilty Spark. She emerged with an intricate knowledge of how the Halo device worked, not to mention a history of the Flood, but whatever else she learned remains unknown. When, in *Halo 2*, she elects to remain behind on a sinking ship, the player would be forgiven for thinking that she is only going to stop the Flood from escaping the Halo; after all, this is what she promises to do. However, in early 2005 it was noticed online that Cortana crosses her fingers behind her back while swearing to destroy High Charity if the Flood get out of control. In the final cinematic, Gravemind meets Cortana in a High Charity that is clearly overrun with Flood. She agrees to answer his questions, although it is debatable as to whether or not she has any other option. Although both parties want the Halos to be disabled, the survival of the Flood will ultimately mean that humanity is consumed by their voracious hunger for new hosts. No alliance can be good for humans.

Bungie

And so we reach number seven on our list of components in the complex mythology Bungie uses to add layers to the *Halo* story. Much of the above relies heavily on the gamer refusing to believe that he has ever completely uncovered something. Whether he sticks around after all enemies are conquered in order to hear a few lines of revealing dialogue or research every possible historical mention of Cortana, there is always something more to be found. Bungie cultivates this sense of mystery with a set of legends that surrounds itself, as well as its games. It has a seven step plan for world domination. Worryingly, steps one through five are already complete, and step six is looking likely. As step seven involves a very big slingshot and the sun, players can only hope that it takes its time and does things properly. The in-jokes woven into *Halo's* infrastructure are amplified by the community that has built up around the game. Similar to a giant game of Chinese Whispers, rumors of an important snippet grow to mythic proportions. The "yellow banshee" is one such example of the gossip mill kicked into overdrive. One sarcastic post about an impossible situation resulted in the white whale of an Internet generation. A poor soul who claimed to have the banshee vehicle in the last level was met with derision and declarations of a yellow banshee. The legend expanded to level walk-throughs and hints about how to obtain one. Some enterprising fans made screenshots of the impossible banshee to further trick the gullible. Still, the only reference in the games themselves is an obscure billboard advertising a yellow car. Nothing is ever as it seems. The Bungie legacy of egotism and complexity leaves the fans always wanting more, and there is usually more to find.

If with these seven layers of myth and legend you are still unconvinced of the levels into which the Halo series can be interpreted, then let me present one last argument. On *Halo's* largest fan site, Halo.Bungie.Org, the "Story and Speculation Page" is listed under "Game Fun." At the time of writing, it has passed 1,000 submissions regarding all aspects of the *Halo* story. Everything from humanity's history to different Covenant factions, Forerunner constructs, and rampant speculation is considered by a team that consists of three active editors and two people with editing privileges. The ratio of actual submissions to those that make the grade could be estimated at anything from one in three to one in seven. None of the editors have the heart to guess. The first submission on January 8, 2002, coincidentally, mentions the collective Bungie obsession with the number seven. The Marathon games have a similar page that has been around since September 1995 and is, as of this date, being updated by the faithful editors who still receive submissions. In fact, *Halo* was first advertised to these loyal Bungie fans almost three years before it was released by means of the "Cortana Letters." These cryptic messages were sent to the maintainer of the *Marathon* story page in 1999. Quickly, parallels were drawn between Durandal and this Cortana, and the letters have been the subject of much discussion. In the recent past, they have been labelled as mere history and not viable story material—a cute way for Bungie to grab the attention of its devoted followers who recognize their content. It has only been since the release of the *Halo 3* trailer that Cortana has shown a resemblance to the Cortana in the letters, going so far as to quote her directly. The term *rampant speculation* would be apt even without the Bungie undertones. The success the Cortana letters have had in infiltrating the public consciousness has been replicated by hopeful interlopers. The Enkidu saga of 2004 seemed like the next generation, but turned out to be an inspired work of fan fiction. Those who were familiar with the Cortana letters knew that they were first considered to be a hoax, anyway, as hoaxes are a long-term hazard of participating in the Bungie community. The story page is not devoid of a sense of humor. For a while, it was speculated that the Master Chief was, in fact, Elvis, and there has always been a connection between the Forerunner and various pastries. Those who have been around the block with the Marathon games are happy to participate and fool the younger kids who have never before seen anything so viral, so wicked, and so engaging. Microsoft even adopted the strategy as an official marketing ploy of *Halo 2*. *The Haunted Apiary* warrants a dozen essays again on its complexities. So confident was Microsoft in the curiosity of the average gamer, that it used the *Halo 2* theatrical trailer attached to the film *I, Robot* to start off the campaign; none of it would have been possible without the fans willing to go out and do the research.

It's all part of the myth.

Jill MacKay is a twenty-year-old student studying zoology at the University of Glasgow, Scotland. When she's not dissecting snails or chasing after birds, she can be found terrorizing literary agents with various unpublished novels. She and her little sister have been tackling *Halo* on cooperative play since 2002 but have still to complete *Halo 2* on Legendary. This is blamed on their aversion to being shot at.

Janine Hiddlestone

IS HALO DOOM-ED?

The Master Chief
Goes to Hollywood

As of this writing, the fate of the Halo *movie is unclear.*
This essay asks the question: Are we sure we even want a Halo *movie?*

IN AN EPISODE in the second season of *Felicity* (the breakthrough television series that would launch creator J. J. Abrams to the successes of *Alias*, *Lost*, and *M:i:III*) one of the characters acquires a video game, much to the derision of his college friends. Noel's attempt to complete the game's quest becomes an amusing subplot in an otherwise serious episode. Eventually, his flatmate Elena joins the game, believing her "superior intellect" will overcome a mere "game." It is interesting watching these two, ostensibly the most intelligent characters in the show, become obsessed over a period of days. They stop going to class, don't sleep, barely eat, and ignore their friends. They make desperate telephone calls to unknown contacts for help, engaging in conversations that make them sound like junkies looking for a fix. They finally get the number of someone who can help them, but when the directions fail, Noel screams at the person on the phone. Bewildered, he hands the phone back to Elena, contemptuously exclaiming, "He's crying!" to which she replies, "Well, he's seven years old!" The game is packed up and put away ("Crash," 2-5).

While that game was by no means as complex or sophisticated as current games (such as *Halo*), it does reflect the stereotypical world of gamers and all that is "bad" about the influence of these games. Video games, like many previous technological advances, are variously considered everything from fun entertainment to the root of all evil. While their benefits are on occasion discussed, games are more often cited as causing obesity, poor grades and social skills, and anti-social behavior including violence. Like all stereotypes, this one contains some basis in fact, though the truth is somewhere closer to the middle. Too much of anything can be bad, and obsession is rarely positive, but—despite the hysteria that has surrounded the industry in recent years—video games do not appear to have produced a population of violent, loner, overweight drones. Many, in fact, have produced a loyal fan base—in some cases, almost a cult following.

Halo is one of these games. Released in 2001 as the signature game for the Xbox, Microsoft's first foray into the game console, it has become one of the bestselling games of its type. Technologically superior to most of its contemporaries, it has spawned not only the expected fan base and spin-offs (books, lore, clubs), but also an expansion of the technology and imagination through machinima—animated films based on aspects of video games and particularly popular among players of *Halo* (Biever). It therefore seems a logical next step to Hollywood and the multiplex, and in fact just such a plan was announced in 2005 for a tentative 2007 (later postponed to 2008) release. While this has indeed induced excitement among fans, there is also a sense of trepidation that expectations will not be met and their game experience will forever be sullied.

These concerns are not without some foundation. It is perhaps no small irony that the film industry is now financially subordinate to that of the video game industry. It is widely accepted that most of the films adapted from bestselling video games have been disappointing, or, as in the case of the highly anticipated *Doom* (2005), disastrous. Even though *Lara Croft: Tomb Raider* (2001) and *Resident Evil* (2002) were financial successes, it could be argued that these films' female stars raised the popularity level—critical success was largely elusive, particularly among those who matter most: the gamers. Even blaming the "Hollywoodization" of the games does not appear a compelling argument when considering the failure of the non-mainstream-produced *Alone in the Dark* (2004) and *Blood Rayne* (2006) to attract cinema goers (The

Numbers: Box Office Data). Two questions raised by this dismal track record are why these movies disappoint their intended audience and whether *Halo* will suffer the same fate.

Since the dawn of the video game era, games have had their devoted fans, but the level of interest and commitment to certain titles has increased incrementally with the complexity of the technology, with one often driving the other (it is no coincidence that most games are designed by gamers). It is difficult to imagine players of *Pac-Man* camping for days in winter for the release of the next version, or spending incredible amounts of time creating back-stories, designing animation, or even joining in online discussions of such depth as to put Oprah's Book Club to shame.

It is not simply the improvement of computer graphics—though that plays a significant role—that has altered the commitment of gamers. Affordability has also been a contributing factor, providing broader accessibility to the mass market (I suspect many of us remember our first *Atari* or, for the very indulged, *Commodore 64*, which were more expensive than contemporary game consoles). But what the advancements of affordable technology have really achieved is the ability to create increasingly complex storylines and characters. This has provided a level of escapism previously unrealized in an electronic form. For some time, politicians, parents, and educators have decried the decline in reading and the loss of knowledge and experience that is believed to be occurring with the drift from the written word. It is these concerns that led to the excitement surrounding the popularity of the Harry Potter books, despite concerns by some religious groups over the content. The near hysteria exhibited over the number of these books being sold made one wonder whether parents wouldn't be nearly as thrilled to have their children buying *Playboy* for the articles, such was their excitement to see the kids reading (no offense to Harry and friends).

However, the increasing complexity of video games has prompted some academics to suggest that games may indeed be the electronic evolution of the book. In his investigation of the computer game as a fictional form, Barry Atkins found that the "player was provided with the building blocks of a story that was 'written' or 'told' through its playing out according to the internal logic of the game. Here was a form of fictional freedom: I could tell the story again and again and bring the story to a variety of conclusions. Here was a form of fictional restraint: I could only tell the story in a particular way" (Atkins 5). And while this will be inevitably debated for years to come, it is true that many of the best-selling games contain plots, dialogue, and characterization of increasing sophistication. There is even a suggestion that some games may encourage creativity by providing the player the opportunity to have a role in developing the story. Stephen Johnson has also pointed to a range of possible enhancements in cognitive skills, among other educational possibilities (Johnson).

This essay is not the place to debate the merits of both sides of the divide in this issue, but it does provide some credence to one of the possible reasons for the difficulty in transferring the game to the cinema. In theory it seems that transferring one visual media to another should not only be done with some ease, but also with general success and a positive reception. However, each new announcement of a move to the big screen is treated with increasing apprehension by disillusioned fans. The reaction is remarkably similar to those of fans of a beloved book that receives the movie treatment. Any doubts about this can be dispelled by Peter Jackson, the director of the most popular literary adaptation in cinematic history, *The Lord of the Rings*. Even with its phenomenal success, Jackson was constantly aware of the repercussions of disappointing Tolkien fans. And although reviewers were generally pleased with the outcome, there was still criticism on a range of issues, including interpretation.

There must surely be few people who have not seen a movie adaptation of a favorite book and been disappointed. Whether from classics such as *The Chronicles of Narnia* or *Doctor Zhivago*, to contemporary bestsellers such as *The Constant Gardener* and *The Firm*, or even *Harry Potter*, there are inevitably aspects that don't translate as expected. These can be individual, or more universal. It might be as simple as the look of the character, or as divisive as huge chunks of story changed or abandoned. Sometimes it is not even that simple, with some critics claiming that *Harry Potter* was *too close* to the book (Turan).

Halo will certainly create differences of opinion. Who should play the Master Chief, and how should he be portrayed? Like a main character in a novel, everyone (and no one) knows what he looks like, but everyone's image is different, as he is a construct of the reader's imagination. This is even more problematic in regard to *Halo*: it is a first-person shooter-style game, and unless playing in a group, the player is always the Master Chief (though in *Halo 2* the Arbiter is also a playable character), so the character structure becomes even more individuated. It is a little easier in the third-person games, such as *Tomb Raider*, but then it was nothing less than unnerving how much Angelina Jolie looked like the character—a state of affairs unlikely to happen often in casting. Blog discussions have suggested that the Master Chief lends itself to a Bruce Willis or Arnold Schwarzenegger type, though both may possibly be too old to play the role. Rumors about Denzel Washington caused controversy between gamers, and casting an unknown brings with it a range of other concerns (Wikipedia, "*Halo* [film]"). There have even been discussions in pre-production about whether Master Chief would be a "guy running around in a suit" or a fully CGI created character (Vespe). Even in a game with less character development, such as *Doom*, casting was difficult (and not assisted by a total lack of apparent acting ability in the leads: "The Rock" was honored with a Golden Raspberry).

And this is all *before* the adaptation process. Will the script follow *Halo 1* or *2*, or a combination, or will it deviate significantly? These are concerns not only among fans, but also creators Bungie Software and Microsoft. A spokesperson for Bungie, citing these issues, suggested/admitted that the movie may be based on the ideas and the environment of *Halo*, but might not necessarily follow the game story precisely (Staten Pt. 1). This has been the form that most recent game adaptations have taken, to varying degrees. *Lara Croft* used sections of games for particular scenes, but storylines were augmented and characters changed to produce a more "complete" story and more "developed" characters. The level of success attained by this strategy is contestable, but the movie certainly found an audience. Reaction to the approach may be more telling from the response to the sequel, *The Cradle of Life*, which earned only slightly more than half of what the first did at the box office (The Numbers: Box Office Data).

Paul W. S. Anderson took a different approach with *Resident Evil*: he made significant changes, but kept the basic storyline and physical parameters very similar to those of the game. The most significant and surprising variation was the introduction of a completely new main character—Alice—who continued as the main character in the sequel, *Apocalypse*, and apparently will again in the forthcoming third installment. There is ostensibly no reason to have created Alice, as she largely follows the role of Jill Valentine (and aspects of Claire Redfield) in the first movie. Even in the later *Resident Evil* games, there is no character that really resembles Alice. *Apocalypse* follows the game script even less closely, borrowing from several of the games. Anderson's gamble paid off financially, with *Resident Evil* doing respectable business and *Apocalypse* doing even better (The Numbers: Box Office Data). Critics were scathing and fans divided, but it did attract non-gamers and converts, which has proved to be the biggest failing of other game-adapted films.

But neither *Lara Croft* nor *Resident Evil* has the personal involvement that *Halo* tends to invoke. This is due not only to the complexity of the story, or its AI abilities, but most particularly to the first-person scenario. It is the latter similarity to *Doom* that is causing unease in the game and movie world: released at about the same time as the announcements for the *Halo* movie deal, *Doom* is the quintessential first-person-shooter and one of the most popular video games ever released. As infamous as it is famous, *Doom* is often demonized among those opposed to violent video games—most notoriously after the Columbine High School shootings (Wilks); the only other game with even close to the level of negative publicity is *Grand Theft Auto*. To describe the movie adaptation of *Doom* as unsuccessful is to pay it a compliment (okay, perhaps that is a bit harsh, but only a bit). Critics, fans, and cinema-goers alike could find few redeeming features, and box-office takings did not even come close to covering production costs (The Numbers: Box Office Data). *Resident Evil* cost half the money to make and received double the takings. To understand the reasons for the failure of *Doom* would take more words than are available here; an entire cabal of therapists will probably be hearing the reasons for many years to come. But the most urgent question (particularly for the *Halo* developers) is was it a bad film, or a bad game adaptation? Even the widely discussed "first-person" sequence, where the movie temporarily lapses into game mode, does not look "clever" or "edgy," just cheesy, cheap, and literally nauseating (though its originality and intent has received praise from some quarters). It would be fair to suggest that *Doom* is keeping many on the *Halo* project awake at night.

The producers stressed that their aim was to stick as closely to the game as possible, with no embellishment or enhancement. Unfortunately, this had the effect of alienating non-gaming viewers who often remained mystified by the storyline. A few critics praised *Doom*'s simplicity in staying close to the game (Hillerstrom), though this approach is seen by critics of other game adaptations as problematic (for example, James Dyer suggested that the biggest problem in *Silent Hill* [2006] was "unwavering fidelity to the source material" [Dyer 25]—proving once again the "damned if you do, damned if you don't" conundrum faced by those adapting games). But staying close to the game was not close enough for many *Doom* fans who were displeased with several changes. They criticized the fact that the focus of the movie was *Doom III* rather than the original; however, their main point of contention related to a significant change in the game's theme (Wikipedia, *Doom* [film]). The source of the threat in the games is known as Hell, who releases great evil. (It is rumored to be a less-than-subtle Christian allegory.) In the film, the threat is a genetic mutation caused by exposure to some sort of viral agent or contaminant (similar to *Resident Evil*). While a number of reasons could be suggested to explain this change, it would make scant difference to the fans.

There are also religious overtones in *Halo* that may present problems in the current political climate. The aliens, aptly named the Covenant, belong to an extreme religious sect that sees humans as an abomination that must be destroyed. The setting itself, the Halo, turns out to be a type of technologically advanced "ark" (albeit extraordinarily large), which both attracts and protects from the one threat to both humans and the Covenant: the Flood, a conscious viral agent that kills all in its path. The player, as Master Chief, a superhuman cyborg, must battle to save humankind. Master Chief is in many ways quite alone—as the rest of his "type" has seemingly been wiped out—but has a group of loyal helpers (all that is required are loaves and fishes and a last supper to complete the story).

It would be wrong to extend the religious theme to the devotion of the fans—though there is an argument to be made for it—but the ardor for which many feel for *Halo* should not be underestimated. *Halo* is more than a game; it has created an entire environment in which it is understood that the events occurring in the game are only a small part. It has spawned authorized novels that fill in a lot of the detail and context that the game cannot, as well as countless other stories published on the Web (and probably elsewhere), not to mention the machinima, which has recently found its way off the Web and onto the screens at film festivals such as the San Francisco International Film Festival (Surette). The wider universe of *Halo* has similarities to the Star Wars franchise, which has inspired a diverse range of spin-offs in which the characters of the films often play minor, if any, roles. And if the fans of *Halo* have even half of the devotion of their Star Wars cousins, the filmmakers will be under considerable pressure.

An awareness of the problems faced by previous game adaptations ("failure" in this context is a very objective term) has led to the creators of *Halo* attempting to follow a different path. Concerned about the aforementioned "Hollywoodization" believed to have caused difficulties with other adaptations, *Halo*'s distributor, Microsoft, has taken two unusual steps. The first was not to sign over the rights to *Halo* without discretion, instead striking a deal in which Microsoft reduced its sale price from $15 to $5 million in exchange for 10 percent of gross profit and some creative control, with the project shared between two studios (Universal and Twentieth Century Fox, which have recently removed themselves from the project) to spread the costs (*PC Magazine Online*). The second was to grant the creator, Bungie, a significant amount of creative participation. Thus far it has included script feedback, meetings with the production team, and the assembly of an encyclopedic publication, covering all aspects of *Halo* from the character to the environment to full specifications on all vehicles and weapons, to help the movie makers "get it right" (Staten Pt 1). (There are entire discussion boards on Web sites dedicated to the inaccuracies of the weapons and other minutiae used in *Doom*.)

Not wanting the script written by any Hollywood insider, Bungie turned to British writer Alex Garland after seeing his work in *28 Days Later* (2004). Garland professed to be a fan of *Halo*, which, according to Bungie, made him the perfect candidate along with his experience. While not to everyone's taste, Garland is a critically acclaimed writer and therefore a minor coup for a game adaptation. Garland's script caused great excitement at Microsoft and Bungie, with claims that "it kept getting better with each successive draft" (Staten Pt. 1), and he was ultimately paid $1 million for the product. Fans were assured of its quality, and the script was delivered to the studios by actors dressed as Master Chief. However, the story of the story has not yet had a happy ending: D. B. Weiss, of whom little is known, has been hired to "rewrite" the script, but is apparently retaining "significant aspects" of Garland's script, with the movie release date being pushed back to 2008 (Halo-movie.trivialbeing.net).

The biggest breakthrough for the project was the obtaining of Peter Jackson and his Weta Studios to produce the movie (Staten Pt. 2). This *should* guarantee a high-quality production, if nothing else, and they know something about adaptations. When this news was announced, there were a series of rumors, allusions, and misunderstandings that led to the reporting in some places that Jackson would direct. Gamers were dancing in cyberspace heaven! When the correction was made public, there was palpable disappointment, but Jackson and Weta's involvement in the project was still viewed as worth celebrating, as they would undoubtedly have considerable influence on the finished product. It did not herald the end of the director dramas: speculation saw the potentials change on a weekly, if not daily, basis. Popular prospects included Guillermo del Torro (*Hellboy*) and Alex Proyas (*The Crow*; *I, Robot*). Less popular ones included Uwe Boll (*Blood Rayne*, *Alone in the Dark*), who, while having considerable experience with game adaptations, has yet to have any experience with a successful film (Wikipedia, "Halo [film]"). It is quite likely that the flurry of publicity surrounding the speculation of his involvement was enough to cause the onset of panic disorders among dedicated *Halo* fans, as he is quite proud of his reputation of being one of the "worst directors in the world" (*Empire* 76–78). The rumor was strongly denied by Microsoft, Bungie, and anyone else with access to a Web server.

In August 2006, it was announced by Xbox.com that South African Neill Blomkamp had been chosen as director and was widely reported on a multitude of fan Web sites. The absence of a denial from any of the major players suggests that it may be true—though no confirmation has yet occurred. If Blomkamp is the choice, then it is an interesting and brave (foolhardy?) one: *Halo* would be his feature film debut, as his previous experience is in commercials and short films. There could be advantages to such a selection—no industry baggage, no comparative expectations, and possibly more control for the producers. He has already pleased many die-hard fans by admitting that, as a fan himself, he prefers *Halo 1* to *Halo 2*, an issue generally agreed upon among fans. But it is an enormous risk to experiment with an untried director on a film involving so much pressure, and, by Blomkamp's own admission, an incredible compilation of resources at his disposal (Vespe). However, one possible reason for such a seemingly wild card choice may lie in the fact that he is not a product of the Hollywood system. Most of the decisions made by Microsoft and Bungie appear to have been attempts to avoid the path of previous game adaptations, even going so far as to choose non-Americans for many of the major development issues, including Weta, which will take the bulk of production (including principle shooting) to New Zealand, where secrecy can more easily be assured.

Ultimately, the key to the success of a *Halo* movie lies with Master Chief, just as it does in the game. Casting may become a non-issue if it is decided that he keep his helmet on for the duration of the film, remaining faceless as he does in the game. Perhaps by adhering to this feature it might allow the fans to continue to see him as they do in their own mind—as themselves—retaining a certain amount of control. This is perhaps the most difficult part of any first-person shooter game to adapt, but it is perhaps even more so to fans; *Halo* is the ultimate quest. In a world where such limited control of the everyday is possible, *Halo* provides an opportunity, for a few hours, to be in control of your own destiny; to be the person you long to be; to right wrongs and be the hero that your faceless job will never allow you to be, in another world where being faceless has the ultimate freedom and power. Accurately portraying the world of *Halo* with its machines, the human "good guys," the mysterious Cortana, and alien enemies of the Covenant is exceedingly important if the movie is to gain the acceptance of fans, but even a perfect adaptation of these things will be meaningless to many if the soul of *Halo*—the hero around which all revolves—does not provide the element of control in the Master Chief that is present in the game.

Unfortunately, this may also be the element that prevents the movie from attracting a non-gamer audience—an important factor in the financial bottom line. If the hero remains faceless, will it be difficult to connect to him if the story is unfamiliar? Emotional investment in a story, particularly one involving a quest, usually requires a bond to be forged with the main character, a situation that may prove uniquely difficult without the expressions and emotion provided by a face. This provides both a conundrum and a challenge to the creators—one that is less reliant on financial resources than it is on ingenuity.

Microsoft, in its first foray into the motion picture industry, has attempted to be creative and original in its approach to bringing *Halo* to cinemas. While a number of these ideas look promising on the surface and have by and large attracted the support of fans, it is impossible to know whether they will have any effect on the outcome once the studios take charge. Game adaptations do not have a good track record, and even those that have experienced financial success have not necessarily been seen as triumphs of the genre. *Halo* may prove to be a windfall for all involved, and, ultimately, this is a marketing opportunity—and strategy—for Microsoft that may well pay outstanding dividends. But for the gamers, the outcome is less certain. Even among dedicated fans, there are only a certain number of points on which they agree; making any attempt to satisfy all of their expectations is perilous indeed. It is quite probable, and indeed unfortunate, that the next point on which they might agree will be on their dissatisfaction and disillusionment with *Halo*, the movie.

Janine Hiddlestone is a lecturer and tutor in politics, history, and communications at James Cook University in Australia. She has a Ph.D. in political history and has published on the place of war in culture and history, and how pop culture became the centerpiece of so much of the public's understanding—and misunderstanding— of events. She has explored the influence of technology on pop culture and vice versa, as well as its pedagogical uses in encouraging students to develop an interest in political and historical issues. She has also attained infamy among her colleagues as a pop culture tragic.

REFERENCES

"A New Writer for *Halo* Adaptation." *Halo Movie.* 17 July 2006.
  <http://halomovie.trivialbeing.net/>.
"*Halo* (film)." *Wikipedia.* 9 Aug. 2006.
  <http://en.wikipedia.org/wiki/Halo_%28film%29>.
"*Doom* (film)." *Wikipedia* 11 August 2006.
  < http://en.wikipedia.org/wiki/Doom_%28film%29>.
"Microsoft Signs Film Deal for *Halo* Video Games." *PC Magazine Online.* 25 August 2005.
"The World's Worst Director?": *Empire,* June 2006, 76–78.
Atkins, Barry. *More Than a Game: The Computer Game as a Fictional Form.* New York: Manchester University Press, 2003.
Biever, Celeste. "The Animation Game: Could Movies Made from Video

Games Soon Have Hollywood on the Run?": *New Scientist* 180: 2418 (25 Oct. 2003): 28–31.

Dyer, James. "*Silent Hill*: Review": *Empire*, Sept. 2006, 25.

Hillerstrom, Oscar. "*Doom*: Review": *Empire*, April 2006, 105.

Johnson, Steven. *Everything Bad is Good for You: How Popular Culture is Making Us Smarter*. New York: Allen Lane, 2005.

"Peter Jackson Comes to Visit." Bungie.net. 7 Feb. 2006. <http://bungie.net/news/topstory>.

Staten, Joseph. "The Great (Hollywood) Journey: Part 1." Bungie.net. 23 Aug. 2005. <http://bungie.net/news/topstory>.

Staten, Joseph. "The Great Hollywood Journey: Part 2–10,000 Pound Gorilla." Bungie.net. 4 Oct. 2005. <http://bungie.net/news/topstory>.

Staten, Joseph. "The Great Hollywood Journey: Part 3." Bungie.net. 1 Nov. 2005. <http://bungie.net/news/topstory>.

Surette, Tim. "Halo Machinima Makes Film Festival." *GameSpot*. 19 April 2006. <http://www.gamespot.com/xbox/action/halo/news.html?sid=6147925>.

The Numbers: Box Office Data. "Box Office History for Movies Based on Games." July 2006. <http://www.the-numbers.com/index.php>.

Turan, Kenneth. "Harry Potter and the Sorcerer's Stone." *LA Times*, 16 Nov. 2001. <http://www.calendarlive.com/movies/reviews/cl-movie000091447nov16,0,1718845.story>.

Vespe, Eric ("Quint"). "Interview with Neill Blomkamp." *Aintitcool.com*. 10 Aug. 2006. <http://www.aintitcool.com/display.cgi?id=24139>.

Wilkes, Daniel. "Training Killers Since 1993 (Doom, video game)": *Metro Magazine*, Winter 2005, 146.

David Thomas

GUN ON A BUN

Halo as Hotdog and the Critics Who Bite

If Halo is a hotdog, what does that make Super Mario? Spam?

IF I WERE A FOOD CRITIC, it would be hotdogs. Since I write about video games, it's *Halo*.

I've never seriously considered writing about food for the same reason I don't write about sex or sleeping or keeping pets. Some things are better enjoyed without a lot of intellectual apparatus to twist them up and make them into a nervous thing. Dogs, after all, bite when they sense fear.

Like most normal people, I love dogs. And, like most normal people, I don't like thinking much about dogs. If nothing else, *Best of Show* made it clear that obsessing about dogs will, at worst, make you crazy, or, at best, the object of ridicule. Dogs just don't offer a lot worth considering. Working for a magazine like *Dog Fancy* must be a peculiar form of journalistic purgatory, worse than slaving away at the dull repetitive work of writing about sports.

This is pretty much what writing about food must be like, as well. And I'm sure this seems like sour grapes to anyone who's never had to produce an assembly line product of criticism, each week, on time, and at the right length, without using swear words, for a newspaper or magazine. In the public imagination, I'm sure writing about food, about eating, must rate as one of the choicest assignments on the planet.

But, from my point of view, no matter how many good meals you get paid to eat, no matter how much you like describing the mouthful of a California Charbono, whatever the appeal of tray after tray of free sushi, Coq a Vin, or Osso Bucca, the reality is that sooner or later you have to write about hotdogs. And like real dogs, what are you going to say? What exactly is worth putting into words about a tube of processed meat on a sweet white bun garnished with the most proletariat of condiments—catsup and mustard?

Where I live, a guy named Biker Jim mans a corner wiener stand where he grills to order all manner of exotics dogs, offers to slather them with onions basted in Coca-Cola and to pump cream cheese into the sausage with a caulk gun. People line up for Jim's dogs, and no food critic, no matter how snooty, can turn away. The average office worker in khakis and a polo could afford to bring a Lean Cuisine to work, or at least spring for a bowl of teriyaki. But instead, they sweat it out in the sun for a chance to snack down on an elk brat with onions and caulk cheese.

This bears scrutiny, and you can't just say, "I'm a food critic. I don't write about hotdogs just because people like them," because your moral obligation runs in exactly the opposite direction. Regardless of your overall interest in hotdogs, whether or not you can tell the difference between a Nathan's Original and a Hebrew National, the fact that lots of people say they care is exactly the reason you have to write about dogs, and write about them like they matter as much as the classiest plates of tapas at some Aspen disco.

So, food critics struggle with the relative merits of hotdogs, and I sympathize, because video game critics have *Halo*. *Halo* is, if you haven't followed the analogy, the hotdog of gaming.

Like some sort of peasant potted-pork product, *Halo* is made of honest ingredients. It's earthy stuff that can sustain you and will probably stop your heart if you're not used to it. But, for all its meat-and-potatoes simplicity, it's hard to say why it's so damn popular. If you're a video game critic, it makes you want to scream. You just can't stand it that this game, of all games, is the one that is supposed to matter. You might as well suggest that *Braveheart* deserves serious film school consideration because it won an Oscar. Somewhere, someone has to straighten out the difference between "popular" and "important." Worst of all, if there's one thing a critic knows, it's that sooner or later, popular and important are the same stupid thing.

This kludge of important and popular shows up in the video game world like this: if a gamer likes a game, they insist that the object of their affection deserves all the adoration in the world because of its "focus on the details." Somehow, in the unspoken rational framework of this assumption, plainness becomes extraordinary because someone worked out the details. In the world of games, there is a strong belief that you can, in fact, polish a turd. And at some magical point it stops smelling and transforms into gold. Game fans, and increasingly the game producers themselves, have bought into the notion of a modern alchemy where the constituent parts don't matter as long as you try hard enough.

That just doesn't ring true for me. Why is *Pac-Man* such a universally popular title? What details did they get right? Are you going to stay up late to postulate that the colors of the ghosts represent different psycho-emotional states that one must overcome in a fit of giant pill-eating? You might as well do a Freudian breakdown of *Gilligan's Island*. Sure, the island represents the mind, with the professor as superego, Gilligan as id, and the Skipper as ego. You can do that. It's a lot of fun with a bottle of good wine and a group of friends. The trouble is, all this waxing eloquent over a bong doesn't do much to explain why people liked the show so much in the first place. It doesn't explain our love of Gilligan, the man-child with the floppy hat. It doesn't explain our fascination with things so obviously unworthy.

So, here's my project—to understand *Halo*. Not to toss off the usual surface gloss on the obvious stuff. Not to suggest that somehow the *Halo* team "just got it right" when it focused on the details. Instead, I want to know why this hotdog of a game is an icon, why it has sold so well, and why, when we hear the onerous tones of the *Halo* anthem playing, we brace ourselves and feel a weird sort of patriotism for the play. You fire up that *Halo* theme in a roomful of people, and everyone who's ever played the game will silently cock a plasma rifle in their mind. Sticky grenades armed, it's time to blow shit up.

But, before we start the frontal assault on the subject of *Halo*, however, I'd like to attempt a critical flanking move, a little covering fire, as it were.

Saying that *Halo* isn't the greatest game ever is a sort of a nerd throwdown indicating that you're looking for trouble. It's the hollow claim of a troll looking for a fight. It looks like all you want to do is make an opening move in a trivial chess game where each turn is a long, dull recitation of game dates and features and explosive proclamations about the relative coolness, say, of the Contra theme compared to the treasure chest opening music from the *Zelda* series. You know, "beep beep beep beep" versus "taladalalda!"

These sorts of conversations never really go anywhere, unless it is toward the goal of making the two guys having the debate that much less attractive to women. And for that reason alone, I don't want to argue the individual merits of *Halo* on some sort of critical matrix.

So, let me say this instead: whether or not *Halo* is the greatest game ever, it probably is not the most interesting game ever. And by "interesting" I mean that any game critic can easily come up with a laundry list of games that are more interesting. Like say:

> *Rez*
> *Animal Crossing*
> *Grand Theft Auto*
> *Katamari Damacy*
> *Parappa the Rapper*
> *Doom*
> *Wario Ware*
> *Everquest*
> *Tetris*
> *Pac-Man*

You get the idea.

Or maybe you don't. So, it's here where we shift into campaign mode and attack the subject head-on. And to do that, I'm going to skip to the conclusion and tell you why critics like to shrug and say "meh" when it comes to *Halo*.

Telling the punch line to the critical joke that is *Halo* first might not sound like a smart move. Really, I ought to spend a lot of time building up to it through a detailed analysis of the game that proves I've spent a lot of time thinking about this subject. And, of course, I need to promise to drop enough inside references and knowing nudges and winks around the structural elements of the game to prove that I have actually played past the first couple of levels. But I just can't think of a reason to withhold the basic reason *Halo* was so freaking popular.

Besides, you already know the answer.

No, it wasn't the music, which was pretty cool. It wasn't the abstract personification of the player as Master Chief, although that was pretty cool. And it wasn't the thoughtful level design, which was, you have to admit, pretty cool as well.

No. Only one thing nudged *Halo* from a good game to a great game in the popular imagination, and that was local area network play. If Bungie hadn't jammed sixteen-player LAN play into the game, we wouldn't even be here talking about *Halo. Halo* wouldn't matter. But they did and it does and we are.

Halo may not have invented the LAN party, but it shaped it as we know it today. Ever after, *Halo* will be remembered as the game that brought boys and their toys together in dorm rooms, apartment buildings, and basement rec rooms like no other video game before or since. *Halo* showed the world that games could be social. And not just social in the weird, people-getting-married-in-the-*World-of-Warcraft* or dressing-like-members-of-a-dwarven-battle-party-in-public sort of way. No, *Halo* presented social gaming as an opportunity for guys with jobs to buy beer and pizza and spend an evening hanging out with their pals. Social gaming existed in the video game world before *Halo*, to be sure. But it was *Halo* that made it normal. *Halo* is one of the few games ever to make hardcore gaming feel middle class.

Let me tell you two stories that help make this point.

I happen to work and teach at a university that offers a pretty sophisticated digital animation program. That means kids come to this school to learn the hardcore nuts and bolts of putting together computer graphics, the kind of stuff used in games and the even more sophisticated stuff they do in Hollywood. These students work on state-of-the art workstations with the current hottest graphics and animation software.

As an after-hours activity one evening, the faculty that runs the animation department got everyone together to play *Halo*. So, a bunch of students lumped their machines to school, networked them through the local area network, plugged the boxes into whatever television or projector they could find, and spent the rest of the evening blasting away at each other.

It looked kind of funny to see ratty Xboxes stacked on top of much more sophisticated graphics hardware. And if you thought about it, it was amusing to watch students, who knew all this sophisticated graphics stuff like surface occlusion, clipping, and spline curves, happily ignore the low-resolution *Halo* graphics they were blowing up on screen.

The word you are looking for is "irony."

You see, they weren't there for the graphics. Instead, *Halo* was speaking to the blue-collar nature of the 3D graphics artist's job. The same way that the guy who runs the drill press down at the shop can just let it all hang out at the Steelers game, just scream and yell and have a hell of a good time, *Halo* does that for the knowledge worker. *Halo* made it okay to just run around and scream and yell and make some noise—ratatatatatatat.

The other story: Bob is the guy you know who likes to talk about computers. Bob is not the computer nerd who writes his own compilers, knows what XML is for, or even writes automation scripts on his Mac to manage his porn collection. Nope. Bob is that guy who built his own PC from components he got at CompUSA, reads PC magazines for fun, and thinks he knows more about computers than he really does.

Bob is also a die-hard Windows fan.

Now, computer snobs (by which I mean Mac users, Penguin Heads, and Open Source Software users) look down on Bob. They mock him for his loyalty to Windows. They try to bait him into conversations about usability or stability, total cost of ownership or extensibility. They goad him on about bloated kernels and undocumented internals.

But all this talk ever does is make Bob sad or mad. It never convinces him of anything except the fact that non-Windows users are jerks. You might as well mock his favorite football team or pick on his girlfriend. His love of Windows is not rational, per se. Instead, Windows is the Ford F-150 pick-up truck of computing. Windows is the stock brand that every man can use and enjoy. Windows is blue-collar technology, and it comes with a certain roughness that means it's authentic, a sort of simplicity that means it's real.

Despite what Apple might have everyone believe, Microsoft is the brand for the rest of us. And when Microsoft got into the console gaming marketing, the Xbox was also instantly the BubbaBox, the game machine that you didn't have to be a gamer to play. *Halo* was just the one cool game everyone told you to buy when you got an Xbox.

Bob bought an Xbox.

So, here's the moral of these stories: While *Halo* was teaching guys that it was okay to get together and play games with their pals, game critics were first amused that the alpha males at work were actually interested in what they, the lowly game nerds, were doing for a living. Then, eventually, the game critics started to sniff at the idea that *Halo* mattered for a very simple reason. And that reason was that when games are successful for social reasons, no one needs the critics.

Go ahead, tell me about the last time you read a deep, insightful, critical analysis of bingo. You haven't, because the act of bingo is not about the game. It's about hanging out with a bunch of other people and feeling a part of something, even if that something is a liturgy of numbers, letter blotters, and a slow hemorrhaging of your retirement checks.

Game critics like to give a nod toward the social aspects of gaming, mainly because if people actually play games to be with other people, then it makes it that much less likely that writing about games means you are a lonely geek who will never find love. At the same time, it's scary to think that people get together for their own reasons and don't care what the game critics have to say.

Look at it this way. Suppose you are in love with someone who's already in a relationship. You can sit there and analyze why she loves him instead of you all you want. At the end of the day, their relationship isn't about you. You're just this outsider who couldn't be more isolated than if the cuddly couple were those freaky weird identical twins who invented their own language so they wouldn't have to talk to anyone but each other. The term "third wheel" is probably one of the worst analogies ever constructed, because three-wheeled things can be pretty stable. So, a better analogy, and one unfortunately not used nearly enough, is "tits on a bishop." Meaning, if you are the third person in a relationship, then you are completely and truly useless.

I imagine that's a little how Mark David Chapman felt when he gunned down John. He knew he'd never matter quite as much as Yoko. And I don't figure that Sir Paul felt much differently.

So, now you know how game critics felt when it turned out gamers were using a game just to see other people.

Unfortunately, being a game critic is a little too much like filling the role of the least attractive girl in the gaggle of the school's prettiest social clutch. Game critics get to feel like they are a part of the inner circle. But a big part of our ability to hang on, tenuously and tenaciously, is that when you are a critic you kind of learn to keep your gripes to yourself and go along with the gang. You may not think *Halo* is that great, but you have to keep that to yourself. Nobody likes a whiny bitch.

So, in time, every critic sucked it up and came to realize that they did like *Halo*. Or least they didn't mind it nearly as much as they might have if not for the growing enthusiasm for the game.

Halo, it turned out, was pretty cool. Everyone said so. And they must have had a reason. People must have had a reason to play *Halo* and not ping pong or poker as their social centerpiece. There was something about *Halo* that was attractive.

Looking back, I think those reasons are pretty easy to sort out: the music, the love of destruction, and the music.

First, the music.

I could argue, like the crusty old video game critic that I am, that the *Halo* soundtrack was an able repurposing of every good idea John Carpenter had about movie soundtracks (which, incidentally, was one). Carpenter recognized that electronic music was easy to make repetitive, and if you made it hurt enough, if the beats just pounded on you like a hammer driving nails, then you'd get uptight, or at least start to feel a kind of thrilling tension.

This is how I account for the fact that the soundtracks to *Halloween* and *Escape from New York* sound more exciting than silly.

Although you might miss this the first time through, *Halo's* soundtrack follows this formula. The main theme comprises a synthesized sound like a whale playing a titanic cello. You could say that the *Halo* soundtrack is almost unmusical sound effects. Like with Carpenter's scores, you respond to the sounds more than the tune. Whatever the case, the soundtrack's particular brilliance is making you feel like some serious destruction is about to take place (which we will get to in a moment).

I'm sure this is a deeply unpopular view, since the *Halo* soundtrack is among the most revered of any video game. But compared to, say, Star Wars, *Halo's* score is not about nuance. It's a battle chant. It stirs the killer instinct (which we will get to in a moment) and, most important, it's emblematic. How else can you explain the time I witnessed an entire auditorium of game journalists emit girly squeaks of glee at a *Halo 3* trailer? Why? It wasn't the content of the video—the boxy form of Master Chief waddling through some unspecified wasteland and observing something that looked kind of like a Dutch architect's idea of a really cool rave set. No, it wasn't what was on screen. It was that music, the *Halo* throb, that cello thing. The room dissolved from a bunch of critical game writers into an auditorium of fans. Everyone was ready to join the battle against the Covenant. If the U.S. Army could distill the magic out of the *Halo* soundtrack, we'd all be that much closer to Plato's Republic and Heinlein's world of Starship Troopers as the only real citizens. We'd all want to fight that bad.

Which brings us to the heart of the matter—the music matters because the heart of the game is the heart of darkness, the desire to destroy.

You could say that *Halo* is about saving the world. But I'd point out that *Halo* is really about blowing things to smithereens. *Halo* was born and bred and polished into a delightful wrecking ball of entertainment.

Think about it. *Halo* was the first game to really make the first-person shooter work on the home console. Yes, *GoldenEye* on the N64 was great. But in retrospect, it was more like a prototype than a final product. Prior to *Halo*, if you wanted to run and gun, you'd do it on a PC. We all assumed that a mouse was the natural interface when it came to massive amounts of gunfire in a 3D world.

Halo channeled the soul of *Unreal* and *Quake* and made them joystick compatible.

In doing so, *Halo* merged the bloodlust once reserved for the computer and eased it into the living room. Now, safely snuggled on a leather sofa, you could bring down holy destruction on a deserving enemy. Why deserving? Well, it's not quite clear at first, but it seems some bug-eyed monsters were trying to crush the earth and we, as the disembodied no-man Master Chief, appeared as humanity's last and only hope.

That's given in the playbook of narrative as reason enough to destroy an enemy by the thousands.

It's not trivial and not coincidence that the Master Chief, your avatar, you, is a cyborg, a killing machine in a very literal sense of the term. Not only does the empty shell of the MC's battle armor allow the player an easy mechanism to identify with the character—after all, since the Chief seems to have no history or personality, the player simply becomes the character—we also have this cultural norm in the endlessly imperialistic and aggressive United States of disassociating from the carnage we cause. We think of it as cute to see military bombers with naked ladies painted on the sides of their warbirds because, well, those are the machines that will carry our boys into harm's way, and if a little cheesecake makes them feel better, then fine. They can have a whole damn Cheesecake Factory if they like. But we'd rather not think about happy faces painted on bombs that will tear through buildings and blow real people into very unsmiling piles of meat.

The Master Chief lets us be the tool of destruction without having to worry much about the consequences of destruction. Remember, we are/ he is a tool built for battle.

This pretty much sums up our somewhat awkward relationship with violence. As far as anyone can tell, humans come built in with a taste for smashing stuff up—people, animals, buildings, ideas, whatever. Most of the time we keep it in check by watching professional football or, say, whittling. Given enough time, though, we find that our taste in dramatic conflict flows easily between real-world politics and fantasy entertainment. How else do you make sense out of cameras on smart bombs and televised video of warfront demolition?

You don't need a Ph.D. in politics, world history, or even media studies to figure out that *Halo* provides a simple allegory for global conflict. In the game fiction, we don't really need to know why the Covenant has it out for humans. That they do is sufficient. We don't know why Master Chief fights with such skill and fervor. He just does. We don't have to morally consider whether or not the game's runty Grunts are some off-world oppressed ethnic minority pressed into filling the role of cannon fodder. We just know that they will kill us if we stand still, and that one well-placed frag grenade provides the best rhetoric available under the circumstances.

If we have the slightest sociopolitical sensibility or an inkling that there are people in the world who would like to destroy us, then we can find our hopes and fears played out through *Halo*'s good-versus-evil set piece. Even if we don't, it's still fun to blow stuff up.

Halo certainly won't go down in gaming history as the title that brought violence to interactive entertainment. Shooting things is just one of the primary colors in the video-gaming palette. The *Halo* designers happened to paint in their picture with a strong understanding that people want guilt-free violence as much as they want guilt-free sex. A mythic outer-space struggle between us and them provides all the reason we need, not just to pile up a body count, but to gloat about it the next day at work.

Some might want to argue that it was really the level design, the variety of enemies, the selection of weapons, or variety of locale that made *Halo* work, the rise and fall of action, the shifting battle grounds, the shuffling of opponents that kept the play interesting. But these are the tricks every writer or filmmaker knows. If you have a good idea—finding love/seeking revenge/saving the world—the rest is just pacing and variety. They are not unique to *Halo*. So, once again, I assert that *Halo*'s theme, its driving force, was a simple delight in violence. And oh, what a delight.

Which brings us back to the music.

It would sell the game's soundtrack a little short to focus on the pomp of the "dut duh duh duh" main theme, because the soundtrack has a perfect musical counterpoint—the chorus of angelic voices. If the thundering main theme is the anthem, the call to arms, then the chorus is the requiem, the spiritual uplift. Together, these aural bookends provide context for the violence. You have a need and then repose, an attack and then a release. Violence surrounded by a context.

And that's pretty much the simple brilliance of *Halo*. The French take what other cultures consider offal, add some butter and sea salt and a few herbs, and create a delicacy. *Halo*'s designers didn't need to find new ingredients in foreign markets. They didn't feel the need to innovate in an obvious way. They took basic stuff, fundamental urges and themes, and prepared them with a masterful sense of balance and taste.

Yes, *Halo* is a hotdog. And people like hotdogs for a reason.

Looking back after the short five years since the game was released, I think that, as a critic, I've been harsh, maybe rash in my leap to unload a clip of criticism on this game. You spend a lot of time paid to have opinions, forcing them out, and sometimes, maybe, you just try too hard. *Halo* snuck by not because its brilliance was obvious, but because it was so under-stated. It was so like other things: if you just looked at the parts, you didn't see anything all that exciting.

At the same time, this reflection makes me think of something I read recently.

Literary mastermind and cultural Lex Luthor Umberto Eco once said, "[B]y any strict critical standards...*Casablanca* is a very mediocre film." As far as I can tell, Eco probably liked the film. He just saw it as it was, or as it now exists in the mainstream imagination.

Last I checked, *Casablanca* was on the top-ten list of the most beloved movies of all time. Ironically, Umberto Eco is on the list of the top-ten most important critics you've never heard of.

And that's why *Halo* and hotdogs, rather than critics, matter.

David Thomas founded the International Game Journalists Association (www.igja.org) to help support the quality and professionalism of game journalism. He also teaches courses on the history of digital media, critical video game theory, and human environments at the University of Colorado. For more information, see www.buzzcut.com.

Dean Takahashi

THE MAKING OF HALO AND HALO 2

And the Birth of the Xbox 360

How Halo *almost didn't happen.*

THE HALO GAMES weren't created in a vacuum. They were tied together with the creation of new hardware. The original *Halo* was hitched to the fate of the original Xbox as soon as Microsoft bought Bungie Software for about $30 million in June 2000. From the very start, the pressure was on the team to make a game that would sell hardware. Microsoft needed a hit for the Xbox in order to stand a chance against Nintendo and Sony. For Bungie, this pressure provided the gist for a creative maelstrom. The team had a very short time to pull together a game that was enormous in scope. And the worst part was that Bungie had to tear up its original work and start from scratch. The schedule for the Xbox drove the schedule for *Halo*—something similar would happen with the launch of *Halo 2* and the Xbox 360. The Halo games and the hardware that runs them have had a symbiotic relationship from start to finish. Both influenced what the other would become.

Halo started as the breakout ambition of a small game company in the suburbs of Chicago. Led by Alex Seropian and Jason Jones, Bungie had created memorable games for the Apple Macintosh and rose to commercial success with a game called *Myth*. The Mac had been good for

Bungie, but its days as a game platform were numbered. The team decided it needed to switch horses. It so happened that Ed Fries, the head of Microsoft's games division, found himself in need of a lot of games at the same time. When Bill Gates gave the Xbox its final go-ahead on Valentine's Day in February 2000, Fries found he had just a year or so to double the number of games in production at Microsoft. His scouts found Bungie, negotiated a deal, and moved Bungie's team to Redmond, Washington. The only negative side-effect was that Fries had to mollify an angry Steve Jobs, who wasn't happy that Microsoft had stolen the marquee developer of games for the Mac. Bungie had to hit the ground running on an Xbox launch title. Jason Jones, the project leader of *Halo*, never even had time to change his car from Illinois to Washington license plates. Much like the original Xbox, *Halo* was ready set go.

Fries had made many other bets, as well. But *Halo* looked to be the most promising. He believed in the team and the game. He had seen how Bungie stole the show at the E3 expo in May 1999. The game started as a third-person, real-time strategy game. As the team revised the game over and over again, they pulled the camera view in closer and closer until it became a first-person shooter. Fries wanted them to remake the game into a launch title for the Xbox. They only had fourteen months—and to convert the game to run on the Xbox, the team had to totally remake its plans.

When Microsoft acquired Bungie, the Xbox had barely proceeded beyond the prototype stage. Nvidia still had about nine months before it was due to finish the graphics chip for the machine. So, the team had to run the game prototypes on standard, personal computers. They also had to remake the control mechanism. First-person shooter titles never worked well on game consoles, which used controllers that you had to hold with two hands. It was far easier to point and shoot at something with a computer mouse, where you could quickly and directly point at your target using a single hand. On a controller, you had to use two thumbs to position a target on the TV screen. Jones's *Halo* team was experimenting with the hardware prototypes and game controllers. After an initial assessment, they ditched the Internet multiplayer game, saving that project for *Halo* 2. They decided that they needed to focus on getting single-player right. In this case, the hardware schedule dictated changes to the content that would wind up in the game.

Without multiplayer distractions, the Bungie team built a single-player game with a strong story held together by dialogue between a Clint Eastwood-style Spartan male warrior and a wise-cracking female computer avatar. The Master Chief and Cortana delivered some comic relief in between the fast action. The story revolved around the conflict between humans and an alien race called the Covenant. The aliens and a powerful artifact were on a ring-shaped planet named Halo. The artifact promised to shift the balance of power in the war, and only the Master Chief—the Spartan warrior—could stop them. The story borrowed from science fiction literature. But it was reasonably original, and Bungie eventually tapped a writer, Brannon Boren, to be the keeper of "The *Halo* Story Bible," a closely guarded document that described the *Halo* universe in all of its detail, from the history of the Spartan bioengineering warrior program to Master Chief's childhood. Another writer, Eric Nylund, wrote a novel, *Halo: The Fall of Reach*, that pulled in the back story. And, most importantly, they had crafted cool weapons, from plasma grenades that stuck to whatever they were thrown at to Warthog vehicles that resembled dune buggies with all of the physically accurate bouncing. Bungie had found the right balance of story and what gamers really wanted.

The team worked furiously. At the GameStock show in March 2001, the press loved the game, particularly the rattling of bullet casings flying out of the machine gun as players fired away at enemies. But at the E3 show in May 2001, the hype started to go downhill. The Xbox prototypes couldn't play the game faster than ten frames per second. It was so slow that those who saw the prototype thought it would never be finished on time. Bill Gates and Steve Ballmer stayed in touch with Fries and both wanted to know when *Halo* would be done. When Bungie's second team finished a game called *Oni* under its obligation to its former publisher, Microsoft transferred the people to Redmond to help finish *Halo*. By the end of it, a team of about fifty people contributed to the game. The game went into certification testing and flew into disk manufacturing. It made it to the stores on time and was available on November 15, the day the Xbox launched.

Halo was action-packed. In the course of a minute, the gamer could do something fun that he or she would repeat over and over and over. The enemies could shrewdly jump out of the way when attacked. There were different kinds of enemies that required different kinds of weapons to dispatch. The player had to impress those watching by doing a little razzle dazzle with the controllers: he or she would have to maneuver the warrior and the point of view of the targeting reticle with the thumb sticks. Then he or she could fire the machine gun, switch to grenades and toss one, shift to a shotgun or load up the rocket launcher. Then the player had to hunt for ammo and the next nest of enemies. This repeat-and-rinse cycle could keep the gamer happy for twenty hours. In the vehicles, the player could knock over objects that had real physics behind them, such as a Ghost motorcycle-like hovercraft that could coast into a group of enemies and knock them over.

And targeting with the controller wasn't so hard after all. Bungie cheated. The team built in a forced, but imperceptible, assist—which made the crosshairs fix a target for a little bit longer than normal—without making the game into a turkey shoot. It took just minutes to become proficient with the controller. The game could combine fast-paced action and skill—a thinking person's shooting game that recalled *Golden Eye 007* on the Nintendo 64.

"We were proud that we nailed the controller," said Pete Parsons, who headed the marketing of *Halo*.

The game also made use of the hard-disk drive, something that Ed Fries had argued passionately to include in the Xbox, despite its hefty $50 cost. The game transferred images from the slow DVD drive to the faster hard disk, constantly caching enough images to keep the game from slowing down. While PS2 players had to constantly wait for new scenes to load, the *Halo* gamers didn't have to wait as long. The game also used the hard disk to constantly store saved games so that players wouldn't have to restart a level from scratch after they died. *Halo* thus exploited what Microsoft hoped would differentiate the Xbox from the Sony PlayStation 2 and the Nintendo GameCube.

All of these calculations paid off. *Halo* became the smash hit of the console, helping to sell 1.4 million units in its first U.S. holiday season. As a first-person shooter, it was critical in pulling over PC fans. It kept on selling well after the console launch was old news, gaining a presence in mass culture like few other games had achieved. Fries had made a lot of gambles in his career. With the exception of the Age of Empires series, none had worked out as well as *Halo* for the original Xbox, partly because the hardware was a perfect match for the game.

Once the Xbox was established in the market, Microsoft's hardware and systems software teams moved on to new projects. J Allard's software engineers were working hard on Xbox Live, the online gaming service slated to debut in November 2002. But in early 2002, a handful of chip engineers and game programmers began work on Xenon, the code name for the successor to the Xbox. They came up with ideas for making the hardware faster and better than the equivalent PCs that would come out at the same time. Chris Butcher, the lead programmer on *Halo*, offered his feedback on the design.

Butcher wanted more memory in the system. And he didn't like some of the choices that the hardware team had made. For instance, the system had only a single memory controller that could control a data pathway from one part of the system to another. The CPU would have to go through the bus and the graphics chip to seek data from main memory. This so-called *unified memory architecture* would save on the costs of having a separate graphics memory, but it would cause a long delay in fetching critical data for a CPU that, with a few cores, could process data a lot faster than it could actually get the data. Butcher feared this design would bog everything down. Adding a new memory controller to the system, however, could complicate things and make the whole system more expensive. The original Xbox used unified memory as well, but in the Xenon architecture, the traffic would be much greater. The CPU could run six simultaneous hardware threads, any one of which could stall the traffic. And the graphics chip itself could also stall things. That was why ATI had proposed using embedded memory, a small amount of memory that the graphics chip could address directly and thus lighten the overall bus traffic. Game developers were also concerned about the small amount of embedded memory. The engineers eventually listened to programmers such as Butcher.

Jason Jones experimented with doing non-*Halo* games. But Alex Seropian, a founder of Bungie, decided he had had enough. He left for Chicago and created another start-up. Pete Parsons, the Microsoft marketer, took over as general manager of Bungie. As work began on *Halo 2*, it was clear that *Halo* was becoming Microsoft's key franchise. Among the fifty projects under development in Microsoft's games group, the next *Halo* became the top priority. While *Halo* had succeeded, most other Xbox games had not. Microsoft sorely needed more hits because it was losing money on every machine it sold. The hard disk drive proved difficult to cost reduce, and Microsoft couldn't sell enough games to make up for the initial $125 loss on every machine. The PS2 was pulling away. By the time the Xbox had sold 1.4 million, Sony had sold more than 25 million PS2s.

Ed Fries had to consider how to take proper care of the company's newest franchise. He wanted to heavily invest in the next game and allow the team to work at its own pace so it could produce the best possible game. But Fries had a natural opponent in J Allard, who was in charge of Xenon's design, as well as third-party game development. As the executive team planned Xenon, Allard urged Fries to put Bungie to work on a new version of *Halo* that would debut quickly and exploit the online gaming features of Xbox Live. Other big companies such as Electronic Arts typically exploited their top sellers with small-scale add-on games known as expansion packs. But Fries believed that if he diverted the Bungie team to work on an expansion pack, it would delay the launch of its next big game. On top of that, if Microsoft milked the *Halo* franchise the way Electronic Arts milked games such as *The Sims*, Fries thought fans would lose their enthusiasm. Bungie's team felt the same way. They belittled a *Halo* expansion pack as "Halo 1.5." To appease the other executives, Fries hired Gearbox, an outside developer, to port *Halo* to the PC.

Allard was upset there would be no *Halo* game for the launch of Xbox Live at the end of 2002. But for *Halo* 2, Fries and Bungie wanted to make a big leap forward. The Bungie team would be preserved as if it were a finite resource, and Fries appreciated the creative element in developing games. By contrast, Allard had always had a software engineering mentality. His products were business tools that always hit their budgets and shipped on time. He felt that brute force could get the games out the door the same way it produced results on server and networking software. Fries had to shield the Bungie team from this pressure.

The work on *Halo* 2 didn't start out particularly well. With Seropian gone and Jones paying attention to other games, no one was taking charge of the schedule for *Halo* 2. But the Bungie team had earned some clout and respect within Microsoft. The game kept on selling, with the numbers topping 10 million games. It was the only mega-hit on the Xbox console, scoring as high as the *Grand Theft Auto* game on Sony's console.

"The cult status, the amount of fan fiction that was being written, the tournaments and *Halo* parties all showed that people cared a lot about the game," said Pete Parsons, the new general manager. "It was striking a chord for people, a pop culture phenomenon."

Ed Fries tried to stay abreast of the development of *Halo 2*, but it was just one of about fifty internal game projects he was responsible for. Beyond that, he also had to oversee dozens more third-party games being made by outside developers and publishers. Bungie's slow start was complicated by a couple of things. While Bungie now had more than seventy people in its studio, a half-dozen veterans took off to join Seropian at his new company. Some team members took breaks, but some of the sound team had to immediately work on localizing the game for different international audiences who were now demanding it. Agents from Hollywood came around to see if Microsoft would license the game as a movie. Joe Staten, the cinematics chief, went to Los Angeles to explore the options.

Parsons saw his job as general manager as being responsible for protecting Bungie so that "Bungie stays Bungie." He and Staten saw Hollywood as a siren call that would distract the company from its main focus on games. Bungie was deep in the process of designing, writing, programming, and thinking. *Halo 2* wasn't making good progress, and that put Ed Fries on the hot seat. The designers of the Xbox 360 platform were speeding along for a 2005 launch. But if Bungie fell behind on *Halo 2*, that would push back the launch of *Halo 3*.

"No one was pulling them together, no one was pushing them," Fries said. The marketing and public relations teams were pushing Fries to make a disclosure about *Halo 2*. They wanted him to reveal more about the game at the Electronic Entertainment Expo trade show in May 2002. But Fries didn't want to promise something too soon. He had heated arguments with other executives about why he wanted to keep it quiet. Producing the game properly meant giving it enough resources with no artificial deadlines or marketing-driven features. To focus too much on an E3 demo would distract Bungie from the game. The predicament was a common problem in the games industry. Electronic Arts typically mobilized its developers to hit schedules, such as coming out with a football game every year at the start of the football season. EA would serialize games such as *The Sims*, which became big hits. EA's games were always followed by sequel after sequel. Fries thought that approach would ruin the Bungie team.

"There was a fundamental difference between a top-down organization like EA," Seropian said. "Bungie was an extremely bottom-up company that focused on making a product as good as it could be."

Fries had directed Bungie to make the original *Halo* ready for the Xbox launch, but now Bungie was a proven team. Yet, it lacked a planning process that set timetables for the future on obvious sequels such as *Halo 3*. But *Halo 2* was an enormous task. The game was more complicated because it had to work with sixteen players on Xbox Live. Bungie wanted the playing to be just as fun online as it was on a couch with friends. The plan for the game was huge, with fifteen levels, each of which was many times larger than the levels in the original game. The script for the cinematic sequences ran many pages, and those sequences would run for more than two hours total in the game. There would be seven times as much combat dialogue in *Halo 2*.

"We don't spend a lot of time thinking about the pressure," Parsons said. "The enormity of the job we are trying to do and the high bar we set for ourselves is enough pressure. It doesn't help anything. This was a huge and enormously complex game. So we said when it's ready, it's ready."

And it wasn't ready for the fall of 2003. The revised schedule meant that Fries had to brace for a showdown. He knew that the delays on *Halo 2* would push back *Halo 3*, and that would screw up the launch titles for Xenon. Without *Halo 3* at the launch of Xenon, Microsoft would sorely test the loyalty of its fans. Fries had to contemplate pushing *Halo 2* from a release in the fall of 2003 to the spring of 2004. Bungie was falling further and further behind schedule. Hamilton Chu, producer of the game, decided to leave Microsoft. Jason Jones took over. To make the new schedule, Jones decided to cut the story in half. The second part of the game would become *Halo 3*. It would leave the game with a cliffhanger ending. Jones said that his team could hit the April 2004 ship date, but he doubted the team would be happy with that product. He thought the whole team would quit after it shipped. Jones asked if Microsoft could hold the game for the launch of Xenon, but no one liked that idea.

"It's important to be ambitious," Jones later said. "Certainly you can go too far."

Fries was in a tough spot. He went back to the executive team and asked if they would delay the game to the fall of 2004. That timing would completely ruin the plan to marry *Halo 3* and Xenon. It also meant that the Home and Entertainment Division would miss its financial target for the fiscal year that ended June 30, 2004. Fries argued that they would certainly meet the plan for the following year.

"We could wait until Christmas 2004, and do the game right, screw the fiscal year, and ship one of the best products ever made," Fries said.

But others didn't shake off the problem that this created for the Xbox 360 so lightly.

"It was unthinkable to J that *Halo 3* wouldn't ship at launch," said one observer. "He had a strong core belief that engineering could be managed."

Around July 2003, Bach put the schedule decision in front of the whole executive team. Fries felt that usurped some of his own authority on product development. Fries liked running his business autonomously. But he went along with Bach's move. Bryan Lee, J Allard, Peter Moore, and Mitch Koch all weighed in. They wanted Bungie to finish the game by April 2004, overruling Fries's arguments that it would destroy the franchise. Bach said that the needs of the platform outweighed the needs of any one game. When Fries left that contentious meeting, he thought for the first time that his career at Microsoft could come to an end. He decided that he would always be under pressure to make the wrong decision: to cut corners. Instead of making the decision in favor of the game, he would always have to sacrifice his principles for some greater good. That wasn't the way that he wanted to run a business, particularly one that involved artists. And even if he won the arguments on this game, he felt that the same issue would come up over and over again. The needs of the platform would take priority over the needs of the product. That was all business. It had nothing to do with art.

"I walked out of that meeting and realized that I might wind up leaving the company," Fries said. "I had been there eighteen years. I could see where the paths went. I could see the roads closing. It was inevitable. I had some hope that something would happen. That was when I was first surprised to discover the inevitability of me leaving. It was a shocking thing. I had never considered leaving before."

At about the same time, Fries found that he had to start cutting back on the rest of his organization. He had to juggle teams between working on titles for the original Xbox and the Xbox 360. He looked at the top teams in the organization, the ones that were succeeding and the ones that were unraveling. Taking Bach's advice to cut back in other areas, Fries started cutting back. Microsoft had bought Rare, but that only meant that there were too many people in the rest of the company.

With *Halo 2*, Fries refused to go along with the executive team's decision to ship the game early. He threw a fit and threatened to quit. He didn't think that he was being a prima donna. He felt the franchises were what made the Xbox special. The creative people couldn't be expected to make artistic sacrifices for the sake of the platform. The shortsightedness astounded him. He got them to reverse their decision, and they allowed *Halo 2* to slip to the fall of 2004. But then Fries had decided to leave the company.

"I knew I wasn't going to do that over and over again," Fries said. "I was in an impossible situation. I was emotionally upset because it was hard for me to leave a group that I had built."

The executive team reversed itself and gave Bungie more time. Peter Moore got up on stage at E3 in May 2004 and theatrically tattooed the *Halo 2* launch date on his arm. Though he won the argument, Fries still left the company at the end of 2004, just after the launch of *Halo 2*. At his going-away party, he received a plaque that listed 120 games that the company had published during his tenure, eighteen of which sold more than one million copies. There would be one more.

The Bungie team shipped *Halo 2* in time to make the final launch date of November 9, 2004. It wasn't on schedule by any means, but it matched the date on Peter Moore's arm. In the end, Jason Jones referred to the process as "assembling a cathedral out of a hurricane."

The game shipped simultaneously in twenty-seven countries and eight languages. *Halo 2* shipped in the fall of 2004 and sold $125 million worth of units in twenty-four hours.

It became the bestselling Microsoft hit of all time, making back its $30 million to $40 million investment many times over. Microsoft's marketers staged a clever viral marketing campaign, ilovebees.com, that had stoked fan excitement. Gaming hours on Xbox Live skyrocketed as a million new people began fragging each other in *Halo 2* matches. And in the fourth quarter of 2004, for the first time, the Home and Entertainment Division that included the Xbox Division made a small $55 million profit. Ed Fries would have finally blown away his revenue targets. That was the last act in Ed Fries's Greek tragedy.

Robbie Bach appointed Shane Kim, who had been Fries's chief operating officer for eight years, as the acting general manager of Microsoft Game Studios.

"It's sad for us," Bach said in a phone call with a reporter on the day of the announcement. "Ed's a great guy. We're going to focus on great game content. Fewer games, but high quality. That's a change that Ed started eighteen months ago."

Fries said at the time some things just weren't right, and that he needed them to be if he was going to sign up for another five years. A few Bungie folks left, as well. Bach later added:

Ed's departure was part of the process of Ed deciding what he wanted to do and how we wanted to run the project. Those things happen. Ed's a great person and we wanted him to be on the project. When someone decides to leave, or you have a hole in the organization, you have to be prepared to fill it. We have to structure the organization so that if someone gets hit by a bus, we move forward. In Ed's case, we changed the organization when he left. Those things have happened on every project I have worked on. People leave for personal reasons and you adjust and deal with it. Ed's tenure was critical. The first Xbox wouldn't have gotten done if it wasn't for him.

Bungie's delays had pushed out *Halo 3*, killing any chance for a debut at the Xenon launch. Kim moved titles such as *Call of Duty 2* into a launch position where *Halo 3* might have been, and he put Epic Games' *Gears of War* into another big scheduled slot in 2006. But *Halo 3* was pushed out until 2007. The Xbox 360 launched in November, 2005, without the *Halo* game that everyone thought Microsoft needed to get it off the ground. The Xbox 360 did well enough without *Halo 3*, but it remains to be seen if this divergence of hardware and the marquee software franchise is a good or bad thing for Microsoft.

This story is excerpted from Dean Takahashi's book, *The Xbox 360 Uncloaked: The Real Story behind Microsoft's Next-Generation Video Game Console*, available at www.spiderworks.com.

Dean Takahashi is a columnist in the business section of the *San Jose Mercury News* and author of *The Xbox 360 Uncloaked: The Real Story behind Microsoft's Next-Generation Video Game Console*, launched in May 2006. He also wrote *Opening the Xbox: Inside Microsoft's Plan to Unleash an Entertainment Revolution*. He currently writes a tech commentary and gadget review column for the newspaper of Silicon Valley. He also podcasts and blogs on video games for the *Mercury News* via Dean & Nooch on Gaming. For most of his eighteen years as a journalist he has written stories about technology and has won several awards. He has written about the video game industry for ten years and the semiconductor industry for twelve years. When he has time, he's an avid gamer. He lives in the suburbs of San Jose, California. His favorite game is *Halo*.

Peter A. Smith and Alicia Sanchez

WARLORDS

How Our Troops Are Taking Halo Seriously

Apparently the military is now using Halo *to train the troops. If only they'd start working on those plasma grenades....*

When the Warlords Enter the Halo

Getting off the plane, this might look like any other small town in the South. The warm air, the sweet tea, and the cheery twang of a stranger's greetings might deceive a visitor to this North Alabama destination. But soon the highway changes from four lanes to six, and as you begin to glance up at billboards, expecting to see advertisements for Coca-Cola and Cracker Barrel, you might be surprised to see signs for Lockheed Martin and General Dynamic instead. This town might be different after all. What kind of place has such a ubiquitous presence of high tech? Huntsville, Alabama: one of NASA's many homes, the place the original Apollo rockets were designed, and the host of this year's Warlords Competition.

Very few people know that an event named Warlords exists, and even fewer people have ever been to one. It is a premiere gaming event, held each year between teams comprised of cadets at the Naval Academy, the Air Force Academy, and West Point. Giving up their Spring Break for a small piece of glory among their peers, each contestant plays with the fervor of a linebacker in the much-lauded Army/Navy game. However, the game here was a first-person shooter (FPS), actually an assortment of them, all with similar play mechanics to *Halo*. Little did these unsuspecting players know that they would soon be getting a lesson in teamwork that would stick with them for the rest of their lives.

Why Should the Military Use Games in Its Training?

What today's military has achieved merely by recognizing the importance of teamwork within its ranks is admirable, but the lessons have come at high expense. Lessons learned from a naval tragedy involving the USS Vincennes paved the way for innovative solutions in team training and for many other challenging needs. In the case of the Vincennes, an Iranian air bus was mistakenly identified as a hostile target and destroyed. This incident was later partially attributed to team climate problems, indicating that while some team members must have known the identification was erroneous, they failed to share that information with their teammates for fear of reprisal in second-guessing their commands. This sparked a task force designed to evaluate "Tactical Decision Making Under Stress" and resulted in a renaissance in teamwork training. The Federal Aviation Administration also underwent a transformation regarding its cockpit resource management after identifying teamwork deficiencies that could lead to tragedies.

The primary attraction of game-based training in the military is cost savings. To understand this, you have to think about how you would train a person to drive a tank. Consider the method your parents might have used when you were learning to drive: giving you the keys and reciting the rosary in the passenger seat as you tried desperately to avoid crashing into stationary obstacles, or, if you were lucky, sending you to driver's ed, where you could crash the school's car into stationary obstacles and save your parents' car and blood pressure level all at once. Unfortunately, when someone crashes into anything in a tank the damage is usually much worse than a few mangled lawn ornaments. So, the military took to simulation, and its collective lawn ornament budget dropped dramatically.

In a tank simulator, crews can practice in mock-ups of real equipment and save on the cost of fuel, wear on the vehicle, and ammunition. It provides a test bed to the users as they interact with their teammates in simulated training events that they might not have a chance to experience because they happen infrequently, are too dangerous, or, more often, are too costly. While simulations are a tried-and-true method for developing both tactical and teamwork skills, fielding a simulator can cost millions of dollars and require the space of whole rooms or even buildings. Enter games, which have the potential to yield similar benefits to simulators, but on less expensive platforms for training, as some can even be run on a standard laptop computer.

While it may be apparent that a game could realistically represent the use of a modern-day tank, the ability of *Halo* to function as a training platform may seem like a bit of a stretch. Most of the technology in *Halo*, while amazingly fun, is not equitable to anything a current member of the military will ever experience. Games like *Halo* are not being played at Warlords because they faithfully simulate real-world tactics, however; they are being used because, no matter what the play mechanics of the game, the multiplayer platform is a perfect setting to learn about teams and teamwork in a quickly evolving dynamic environment. While games can serve as effective practice environments, allowing individuals to experience situations they might not be able to otherwise, they also provide opportunities for teams to utilize and expand their teamwork-specific skills. High-stress or high-pressure team situations can be simulated within games like *Halo*, and the team lessons learned there can be applied to a team's real-life interactions.

For example, geneticists use fruit flies to study generational mutations based on environmental changes. They seldom, if ever, study humans in the same way they study these flies. The reason behind this has little to do with protecting human subjects and almost everything to do with the fact that humans live too long. Identifying the effect of environmental changes takes generations in any species. In humans, these changes occur every twenty to forty years; in fruit flies, generations change in twenty to forty hours, so many more data points can be collected in the same period of time. Similarly, *Halo*'s multiplayer platform provides an experimental environment for team building that lasts only a few hours. Compare this to the project cycle found in industry or the mission structure followed by soldiers, which often takes months or even years. *Halo* teams are the fruit fly version of military teams.

Halo is already being used by many of today's soldiers. A recent article in the *Washington Post* highlighted how *Halo* provided training opportunities to soldiers stationed in Iraq. These soldiers played *Halo 2* in their downtime and were able to transfer lessons learned in the game to their daily operations in Iraq. One soldier was quoted as saying, "The insurgents were firing from the other side of the bridge.... We called in a helicopter for an air strike.... I couldn't believe I was seeing this. It was like *Halo*. It didn't even seem real, but it was real" (Vargas A01). David Bartlett, the former chief of operations at the Defense Modeling and Simulation Office, elaborated: "The technology in game has facilitated a revolution in the art of warfare.... When it came time [for a soldier] to fire his weapon, he was ready to do that. And capable of doing that. His experience leading up to that time, through on-the-ground training and playing *Halo* and whatever else enabled him to execute. His situation awareness was up. He knew what he had to do. He had done it before—or something like it up to that point" (Vargas A01).

But before running down to the mailroom and asking all of the employees to join you in a *Halo* match, it is important to understand why team building and teamwork training is so important. A team's performance is often the result of two main factors: task work and teamwork (Cannon-Bowers & Salas). Using *Halo*'s single-player mode, individuals can hone their task-related skills rather quickly. If, however, you were to form a team of the very best *Halo* campaign players, you probably would not be forming a high-performing team. Teams develop and become high performers through interdependent interactions between themselves and others within their teams and their ability to coordinate their actions, communicate with one another, and allocate their resources appropriately. Behaviors and skills that can be considered beneficial to teams regardless of their purpose are generic teamwork skills. *Halo* multiplayer is especially well-suited to train generic teamwork skills by providing players with a multitude of opportunities to interact as a team. From one player driving a Warthog with another manning the gun, to teams breaking off into offensive and defensive units to capture the flag, the opportunities for team development are abundant.

Halo and other FPS games can create opportunities for interactions between multiple individuals in order to accomplish missions and objectives. Through repeated exposure to varying situations, a new team reduces the learning curve often associated with high-performance teams. Knowledge of both teammates and teamwork can increase performance for teams. For example, new experiences often get assimilated into an individual's mental models, or schemata, of the world. The more experiences an individual has, the more abstract these mental models become, allowing flexibility in the application and assimilation of experiential knowledge. With teams, the more experiences they have together, the more closely aligned their mental models can become. Members of a finely tuned and well-practiced team are often able to anticipate one another's actions, to understand their strengths and weaknesses, and to predict their chances of success at any given task.

Teams who practice as a team are likely to be more effective teams. *Halo* provides an opportunity for teams to practice their teamwork skills in a situation that is, for most, much different than their everyday team environments. Teamwork behaviors like providing backup, self-diagnosing, and peer mentoring stem from individual team members' knowledge about their own skills as well as the skills of their teammates. Cues as simple as a slightly elevated tone of voice are sometimes enough to tip off a highly trained team that one of its teammates is in need of help. This self or team efficacy can be developed through repeated exposure to varied situations in which team skills are necessary for success.

In Gee's 2003 book, *What Video Games Have to Teach Us About Learning and Literacy*, he theorized that an individual's embodiment (or character) within a game is often a reflection of his or her real self. Following this argument, behavior within a game should not greatly differ from behavior in the real world. In *Halo*, for example, teams must share the limited resources available to them. Observing behaviors associated with how those resources are allocated by one team member might provide other members with valuable tacit knowledge that could be indicative of that person's real-world behaviors and beliefs. Each interaction between team members in a team capacity provides an opportunity for team members to learn about their teammates and their preferences, tolerances, attitudes, and behaviors.

Communication among teammates is critical in any type of team, whether it be military search-and-rescue teams, emergency room teams, or advertising teams. This generic teamwork skill can be practiced and improved no matter what the applied task is. *Halo* does an excellent job of helping team members understand methods of communication, from using appropriate phraseology to knowing what information is relevant, when to pass that information on, and to whom to pass it on. *Halo* team players use headsets to communicate with one another during the game. This requires interpretation of verbal commands, which can become difficult during stressful situations. Players must learn to take turns speaking, ensure that their speech is intelligible, and listen for information that might be relevant to them.

Generic teamwork includes collective orientation, an attitudinal component of teamwork that provides insight into the attraction of team play for individual players. Collective orientation also refers to the belief that team goals are more important than individual goals. This is often evidenced in games such as *Halo*, where one team member might sacrifice him or herself in order for the rest of the team to be successful. For gamers, this is just good strategy, setting a trap for the enemy by having one team member serve as bait. In a real-world military training event this might be an unacceptable activity, or against standard procedure, at a minimum. However, every good *Halo* team knows self-sacrifice for the greater good leads to victory.

Team cohesion, or the desire to remain a member of a team, is also evident in *Halo*. Some teams have remained intact since the game's original release, demonstrating high cohesion; their members have remained constant and become an integral part of their team's successes and failures. This internalization and personalization of the team provides motivation for individual members to perform at their best. In many games, personality can be injected into the character's appearance, advertising to some degree a player's attitude and preferences. In *Halo*, each player's color emblem, handle/alias, or player model may be set and appear identically to all other players within their team, which advertises alliances and can deepen their level of commitment with their teammates.

Good teams often perform after-action reviews or debriefs regarding their triumphs and failures, which provide learning opportunities in order to advance their teamwork understanding. While this often happens informally in chat rooms or on social occasions, this type of review has shown to be largely beneficial for both generic teamwork and task-specific skills (Smith-Jentsch, Zeisig, Acton, & McPherson). When teams begin to rehash their experiences, it facilitates the transmission of expectations and perceptions to their teammates. Often teammates share tricks, advice, and feedback regarding performance with one another. This can increase individual understanding of both their team-mates' strategies and approaches, and it can also increase their ability to diagnose and self-correct the team's behavior by providing a non-threat-ening learning experience.

Motivation factors cannot be marginalized when training is con-cerned; therefore, the most effective reason to use *Halo* for team train-ing lies within the medium itself. *Halo* is a game. Games are inherently interesting, motivating, engaging, and in most cases, fun. And the more people like doing something, the more often they are going to do it. The more they do it, the better they are at it. In fact, increased time on task has been linked to increased team skills and team performance (Garris, Ahlers, & Driskell). Complaints about training or learning too much are not likely to be voluminous if the participants are enjoying them-selves, so using *Halo* to teach teamwork can often be a positive experi-ence for both teams and their organizations.

A game's ability to engage its users can also impact its ability to serve as a training tool. While engagement can be linked to several types of experiences, such as immersion or presence with and within a game, en-gagement should also affect an individual or team's commitment. When players are engaged with a game, they internalize the consequences and rewards associated with game play. This internalization of their suc-cesses or failures within a game like *Halo* raises the stakes of their game play and can often serve as a motivator to increase their performance through individual and team learning.

And the Winner Is...

In the end, one team reigned victorious over the others at the Warlords Competition. Without a single defeat, this team stood out as the clear champion of the day. The Army's West Point Cadets had won even be-fore the last round of the tournament.

It wouldn't be fair to say the Army won without qualifying it with the fact that Army training is much more in line with the tasks required of a player in an FPS multiplayer game, possibly giving it an advantage. Also, West Point has a gaming lab in which students are required to play to graduate from the school. They use a multitude of games that train different types of tasks, such as tank driving, urban warfare, and generic teamwork skills. This liberal philosophy on gaming makes being a good gamer part of the West Point culture. In an environment where being a good gamer is valued, they clearly should have the best gamers.

The Army players, were not, however, the best players in the competition. Several of the Air Force and Navy players were actually more skilled individual game players, demonstrating expertise in their tasking. Their teams lost, but not by much. What the Army had that the others didn't was an experienced team. Its team had practiced and planned for the event together, which suggests it was more adept not only at the games, but also at teamwork. The Army team had spent time with the games and played through scenarios, discovering areas to take cover, the best locations to plant snipers, back entrances into enemy bases, and any possible exploits that the enemy would not be aware of.

It followed practice up with a plan. The Army team had distinct maps of each level with paths and tasks planned for each player. No other team had a clearly defined strategy, although they were all experienced gamers. For some participants, it was their first time playing with their teammates. This suggests that even though they were prepared for the task-related work they encountered, they had not developed interdependent relationships with each other and were less able to coordinate and predict one another's behaviors.

Observing each team while moving from room to room, we could sense a palpable difference in energy. The Air Force and Navy rooms were completely silent; each player was acting as an autonomous unit, as if this game of capture the flag was just another round of Slayer. In the Army room, however, the players were abuzz about where enemies were located, who had which area, and who was alive, dead, or badly hurt. All of the Army team members participated in the discussions, each sharing their unique perspectives on the situation. They communicated ideas on the fly, adapting as they played. They acted like a team.

The Army players even assumed team roles before each match, with one player acting as a leader. The leader would spend much of his time watching the action and helping to guide other players to their desired locations. Others would become snipers and proceed to high ground, while others would begin the trek across the map to attack the enemy base. The precision with which the Army team defeated its opponents was an amazing sight to see.

Conclusions

Leaving Huntsville, it became clear that this town was much more than expected. Currently, a large level of prejudice exists against the "games for training," or "serious games," movement. While this is not uncommon with disruptive technologies, it does provide challenges in progression through innovation. Simulation faced similar scrutiny when it was introduced but was able to overcome its detractors by consistently proving itself over several decades, despite discouragement from people who based their careers on trumpeting the praises of live training. History may repeat itself now, as simulation companies and training facilities do battle over the use of lower-cost PC solutions that include games like *Halo*. Cesar A. Berardini, of Team Xbox, noted a special press release made by the Army when the military's stock of *Halo 2* sold out at its Exchange. He proclaimed, "[T]he U.S. Army running out of *Halo 2* is as critical as running out of ammo" (Berardini).

While games are gaining ground in the PC simulation market, they are not commonly accepted as a new way to train. Their limitations regarding their dissimilarity to most real-life events cannot be overlooked, but their utility does give reason to consider researching and eventually adopting them on a large-scale basis. *Halo* multiplayer is a prime example of the potential games may have to serve as ubiquitous training solutions that trainees will want to use without much external prodding. The value of self-motivated and desirable training is something that cannot be overlooked by the military community. Though only a part of the training experience in any field, the teamwork experience that could be gained in a day of playing *Halo* could amount to a more meaningful experience than a week or even a year in a real-world training environment. The bottom line is...games like *Halo* are economical single-serving training tools.

Peter A. Smith is currently working as a visiting professor and research associate at the University of Central Florida, while pursuing his Ph.D. in modeling and simulation at the same university. He was formally trained as a computer engineer and has spent much of his career working with serious games and simulations as a contractor with SAIC and the U.S. Navy. He is also the community manager for the Serious Games Initiative and a blogger for the initiative Web site as well as the Second Life Insider.

Alicia Sanchez is currently a serious games researcher at Old Dominion University's VMASC. Prior to joining academia and completing her Ph.D. in modeling and simulation at the University of Central Florida, she spent several years researching teams and teamwork for the Naval Air Warfare Center Training Systems Division.

REFERENCES

Berardini, C. A.. "Army Runs Out of Halo 2." Team Xbox. 22 Nov. 2004. <http://news.teamXbox.com/Xbox/7256/Army-Runs-Out-of-Halo-2/>.

Cannon-Bowers, Janis A., and Eduardo Salas. *Making Decisions Under Stress: Implications for Individual & Team Training.* APA: Washington, D.C., 2003.

Garris, Rosemary, Robert Ahlers, and James E. Driskell, "Games, Motivation, and Learning: A Research and Practice Model": *Simulation & Gaming 33,* 4 (2002): 441–467.

Gee, James P. *What Video Games Have to Teach Us About Learning and Literacy.* Palgrave, Macmillan: New York, New York, 2003.

Smith-Jentsch, Kimberly A., R. L. Zeisig, B. Acton, and James A. McPherson. "Team Dimensional Training." In J. Cannon-Bowers and E. Salas (Eds.), *Making Decisions Under Stress: Implications for Individual & Team Training.* APA: Washington, D.C., 2003.

Vargas, J. A. "Virtual Reality Prepares Soldier for Real War: Young Warriors Say Video Shooter Games Helped Hone Their Skills." Washington Post, 14 Feb. 2006, sec. A01.<http://www.washingtonpost.com/wpdyn/content/article/2006/02/13/AR2006021302437.html>.

Nick Mamatas

RUN AWAAAAAY!

Playing Halo
the Guerilla Way

Why you don't want to play Halo *with Nick Mamatas.*

HALO IS ONE SMART GAME, especially for a first-person shooter. The genre generally hasn't evolved much since the old analog editions. Ever shoot a pop gun with cork bullets at a plastic duck at the carnival? First-person shooter! What video allows for is armed ducks that shoot back. What *Halo* allows for, and what makes it a superior first-person shooter in a very crowded market, is that the ducks truly seem to *want* to live. The combat AI, both as it motivates Covenant forces and other baddies and as it fuels the decisions of your fellow Marines, is the best in gaming. But that only means that it's not quite as smart as the dumbest soldiers ever fielded.

And that's a good thing, as that is what makes the game playable. No matter what Master Chief's reputation, you-as-he enter the game with a pistol. That's not smart. *Halo's* other brilliant innovation is the introduction of encumbrance—you can only carry two weapons at a time. No more BFGs and chainsaws and rocket launchers and grenade slingers *all* available at the click of a mouse. But the conventions of the genre: aim and shoot and run, run, run, put a severe upper limit on the amount of intelligent play one can bring to the game.

On the ringed world of *Halo*, the best bet *would be* to be a guerilla, if not for the fact that the game's conventions are too closely tied to the worlds of *Doom*, *Quake*, and other, older first-person shooters. As recent world events have shown us, the most firepower doesn't necessarily win the day. Facing American and Israeli combined-forces attacks and high technology, teenage men with RPG launchers, cell phones, and area knowledge have held their own in Iraq, Afghanistan, and most recently, Lebanon. Guerilla war won the day for the VC in Vietnam, and even the American Revolution used guerilla tactics, though it was not a full-fledged guerilla war.

Here's Mao on guerilla war:

> The matter of initiative is especially serious for guerrilla forces, who must face critical situations unknown to regular troops. The superiority of the enemy and the lack of unity and experience within our own ranks may be cited. Guerrillas can, however, gain the initiative if they keep in mind the weak points of the enemy. Because of the enemy's insufficient manpower, guerrillas can operate over vast territories: because he is a foreigner and a barbarian, guerrillas can gain the confidence of millions of their countrymen; because of the stupidity of enemy commanders, guerrillas can make full use of their own cleverness. Both guerrillas and regulars must exploit these enemy weaknesses while, at the same time, our own are remedied. Some of our weaknesses are apparent only and are, in actuality, sources of strength. For example, the very fact that most guerrilla groups are small makes it desirable and advantageous for them to appear and disappear in the enemy's rear. With such activities, the enemy is simply unable to cope. A similar liberty of action can rarely be obtained by regular forces.[1]

This doesn't completely apply to *Halo*, of course. In the game, humans end up invading alien territory after a fashion, so the game doesn't completely replicate an insurgency or resistance against imperialists. However, *Halo* does provide for three alien groups—we're not fighting a committed front. And we must remember Mao's dictum: some weaknesses can become strengths. While blending in with and gaining the support of the natives is essential for some guerilla forces, historically, attachment to native populations has made guerilla wars futile exercises. Prior to the twentieth century, most guerilla wars were non-starters.

---

[1] Mao, Tse-tung. "The Strategy of Guerrilla Resistance Against Japan." *Guerilla Warfare Online*. <http://www.marxists.org/reference/archive/mao/works/1937/guerrilla-warfare/index.htm> 3.

All the aggressor would need to do was march into the towns and villages associated with the guerillas and kill every single human there (and all their livestock for good measure). Only a few killings, merely *some* terror: those are just recruitment tools for guerillas. Genocide is all that ever sapped their will to fight, and back when genocide was a politically plausible strategy during war, guerillas had no chance. No population, thought the hegemons, no problem. Luckily in *Halo*, there's no home or hearth to protect.

But the Master Chief is not alone; there are plenty of Marines scattered throughout the game to help him, and the small groups work well as guerillas. Tactical choices even expand guerilla options. Liberate a Scorpion tank and you can carry other Marines with you, turning the AI from an opponent into an ally. Use the Banshee and you can attack from the air, and better avoid the scut work of ground encounters. Indeed, you can even skip ahead of otherwise inevitable fights, as *Halo* is remarkably open-ended. As game critic Joe Fielder put it, instead of performing missions to get to an end-state, "*Halo* . . . sets you in an environment and expects you to think on your feet and react to a series of quickly changing, hostile situations."[2]

Like guerilla war.

Regulars already use video games to hone their skills. Supposedly, the 1980 arcade game *Battlezone*, a tank game that was also one of the first first-person shooters, made a big enough splash that the Department of Defense commissioned Atari to build a superior version for tank training. According to *Jane's Defence Weekly*, as many as 100 video games are already used for training across the U.S. armed forces.[3]

And video games already serve propaganda purposes as well. *America's Army*, launched in 2002, is an interactive recruitment station with millions of registered players. Once in the actual service, a recruit might get some rest and recreation via Xbox training centers, which the Air Force spent $200,000 on for its European bases.[4] But don't bother going rogue if you happen to be playing one of the military's own games, like *America's Army*:

---

[2] Fielder, Joe. "GameSpot Review: *Halo*." Game Spot Online. Nov. 2001. <http://www.gamespot.com/Xbox/action/halo/review.html?page=3&q=&q=&q=&q=&q=&q=&q= 9> 3.

[3] "Press Centre: US Armed Forces Invest $120m in Video Games." *Jane's Defence Weekly*. Online: http://www.janes.com/press/articles/pc051213_1.shtml 13 December 2005.

[4] Schonauer Scott. "XBOX Fever Hitting Europe Troops Hard." *Stars And Stripes* (European Edition) July 7, 2003, p. 1.

Any gamer who logs in to cause havoc by shooting at fellow members of the special operations team gets kicked out of the game. The joke is they can still log in—but their point-of-view is locked behind bars in the Fort Leavenworth military prison.[5]

There is no gratuitous violence in these games, "[b]ecause the Army would never do that" (Brenzican 6). What use is a virtual reality immersion if one can't beat people to death with one's bare hands, drop a daisy-cutter bomb into a crowded apartment block, or just kick back and smoke weed till it comes time for your commander to need a good fraggin'?

Halo, on the other hand, is far more open-ended as a game. One doubts that the Department of Defense would get a lot of positive results out of training soldiers with it,[6] but it does serve as a good field example from the point-of-view of a guerilla. In the same way the Department of Defense screened *The Battle of Algiers* (a classic film showing how the French were defeated in their colonial holding of Algiers, despite having a massive advantage in technology),[7] it is worthwhile to play *Halo* to get an understanding of fighting an insurgency.

For example, in *Halo*, retreat is often a major part of the game. This isn't necessarily a gamer's instinct, but in a battle with political goals, retreat is essential. The American Revolution was won thanks to General George Washington's embrace of retreat, a classic guerilla tactic. The Battle of White Plains, for example, was a fairly minor battle in the American Revolution. It took place on October 28, 1776, and ended with a colonial retreat. Casualties were light on both sides, but in some ways the battle was a turning point—most believe that General William Howe, with the assistance of Hessian mercenaries, could have ended the war by destroying Washington's army, had he just pursued them rather than pausing to set up artillery.

Washington himself understood what was happening. The British were settling in for winter, even to the point of allowing the war to continue. His strategy was thus to trade land for time, a classic tactic that has been used till this very day... remember how pleased the Bush administration was when it took Baghdad in three weeks and was able to

---

[5] Breznican, Anthony. "Army Recruiting through Video Games." *Washington Post*, 23 May 2002.

[6] For a contrary opinion, see Peter A. Smith and Alicia Sanchez in this volume.

[7] Ignatius, David. "Think Strategy, Not Numbers." *Washington Post*, 26 Aug. 2003, sec. A13.

proclaim "Mission Accomplished"? The U.S. still "holds" Baghdad four years later. Or does it?

Howe and the British, for their part, were also clever not to let White Plains devolve into a general engagement. Howe had his eye on the weather and was looking to control the Hudson, which would allow for the free flow of troops and material down the Northeast Corridor. And Washington, too, knew what he was doing:

> American defeats at Brooklyn, Kips Bay, White Plains, and Forts Washington and Lee compelled Washington to move the remnants of his disintegrating army to the south and west where he could use the Delaware River and its surrounding tributaries to his advantage. Washington was confident that he could outmaneuver the British and their Hessian mercenaries using the skills of the Marblehead Mariners. He remembered well that the intrepid seagoing unit from Massachusetts had saved nine thousand of his men with a successful amphibious rescue along Long Island's East River in August. The Delaware River, he decided, would serve as his base of operations and first line of defense.[8]

This is one of the secrets of guerilla warfare. Don't fight. The Vietcong's National Liberation Front (NLF) generally attacked in small cells, and only when those small cells were sure of *winning* (defined as not being annihilated). They used night attacks and depended on their awareness of the terrain, the support of the peasantry, and silence. To begin with, the NLF hardly had any firearms and used machetes, spears, and daggers. In 1964, the U.S. Army performed a survey of weapons captured along with NLF forces. Ninety percent of them were American.

Sound familiar? It should. There's a segment in *Halo* where such choices are made. You come upon the barracks, and everyone within is asleep. Fire a pistol and you get one kill, but the rest wake up. Use a grenade, you kill a few, but wake everyone else up. Hell, go ahead, use the rocket launcher. You've got savepoints. Or, play like a guerilla and quietly bludgeon the sleeping opponents to death, one at a time.

Reading the FAQs and walkthroughs for the game are handy from the point-of-view of the guerilla fighter. Video games are complex enough that we can no longer consider reading strategy guides or online, fan-col-

---

[8] M. E. Telzrow, "The 'Old Fox' Fools the Hounds: General George Washington, Referred to as the 'Old Fox' by Britain's Lord Cornwallis, Employed Innovative Measures to Outsmart the British and Win the Battle of Princeton." *The New American* 21 (26) 2005: 37.

lected tips as cheating. It's just a matter of replay value. And unlike the closed-down game *America's Army*, which is designed to encourage structure and obedience, *Halo* is full of hidden possibilities. Like guerillas, we share information. The Invisible Elite are hard to kill, because they're, you know, invisible. A bit from one of the many *Halo* FAQs tells the tale:

> INVISIBLE ELITE (according to Element322@aol.com and Rayden Cheung is the Silver Elite on Level 3 after you board the ship, possibly only on Legendary): The most annoying of all, they are totally invisible from long distance, and hard to see even up close! Your best bet is to use an Assault Rifle to guess where they are because when you hit them, you can see them for a few seconds.

> Halo_Sniper2005@msn.com has a strategy for the Invisible Elite: If you use 2x Magnification on the Sniper Rifle, you can see the ripples that they make. You can shoot them then.

> Author's Note: Pistol works, too, but Sniper does more damage.[9]

And there you see the basics of guerilla training. There's no central authority or leader dictating tactics, but rather a shared experience being spread by partisans for the mutual benefit. The first contributor confirms the existence of an enemy weapon previously only believed to exist, the second has discovered (likely after great, if virtual, military cost) a weakness, and a third has determined a secondary weakness. This is how insurgent guerillas collect information and improve tactically in the real world, as well. As the *Defense News* explains:

> Initially, IEDs [improvised explosive devices] were constructed by former Iraqi Republican Guard or Special Republican Guard soldiers. That skill has spread throughout the country over the past two years. According to Army intelligence officers, outside expertise also has come into the country, both from Hizbollah, which has extensive bomb-making expertise, and from Iranian intelligence. Bomb-making skills proliferate rapidly among IED cells in Iraq via the Internet, used by insurgents to share skills. The insurgents' technical proficiency has increased over time with experience.[10]

---

[9] Phill, Justin. "FAQ: *Halo* Combat Guide, Version 2.1." 2 Sept. 2004. <http://db.gamefaqs.com/console/Xbox/file/halo_combat.txt.>.

[10] Cited by Alexander Schellong. Online: http://www.iq.harvard.edu/blog/netgov/2006/03/brinto_milward_on_dark_network.html. May 15, 2006.

Halo is thus smart in two ways. Many games insist that you solve the puzzle during the puzzle-solving times or make you be stealthy when it is time for a stealth-related challenge. Indeed, for so long I found video games virtually unplayable because the actions allowed were so tightly constrained. *Halo* was a revelation. Not since the days of ASCII nethack could I just kick down doors (or blast down doors, or turn into a monster that can slide under the door or pass through walls or eat the door) instead of searching everywhere for a key. *Halo* doesn't involve the magic of a *Dungeons & Dragons*-type setting, but goddamnit, if I have a flying vehicle, I should be able to fly over enemies and go someplace else entirely, without being forced to slog it out in a fight with them because I need to "clear levels" before moving on. And for the most part, playing *Halo* I am free. I can play like an Iraqi insurgent, not just like a U.S. soldier who'll automatically and magically end up in prison for doing "the wrong thing."

Only for the most part, however. *Halo* is still a game designed to be played by people who don't understand, and who have never understood, guerilla war. I speak, of course, about Americans. Though the Revolutionary War involved guerilla tactics, it was never a full-fledged guerilla war. And the U.S., in its various defeats and draws across the latter half of the twentieth century and in these first years of the twenty-first, has always run afoul of guerilla wars.

Technology isn't the answer to a guerilla campaign. You can see just how far you can get with two weapons and some teamwork against an entire armada in *Halo*. Indeed, sometimes the secret to facing a high-tech threat is to go low-tech. The rifle as a bludgeon, or, in Iraq, a thin plate of copper over an old land mine, and even a tank can be punctured—the explosive force turns the plate into a superheated needle—and then turned into a baking pot for the troops within. Hammering copper into plate is a very old technology. Ever hear of the Bronze Age? The higher the tech goes, the lower the guerilla response. How to avoid the unmanned attack drones that fly over the streets of cities in Iraq? Duck under a doorway when you hear one nearby. Even cheaper than the Cu Chi Tunnels used by the VC to avoid detection during that conflict.

Halo doesn't entirely mimic this reality. It's all about getting the larger weapon, the ability to kill more adversaries more easily while running through the levels. A real guerilla warfare game would involve endless amounts of waiting around in a dark room (turn down the brightness on your monitor?) and occasionally haggling for a piece of copper wire, a car battery, some blasting caps, and water. Lots of water. Not a lot to do all day but keep hydrated and wait.

Wait in the cellars, while the boots of the invaders go tromping along overhead while your mother and your younger brother cry and yelp. Something breaks with a crash. More boots. You wait. Not that night; it would be too obvious. Give it four or five days. Maybe your brother, if he's still alive and relatively unharmed, will scout out the local barracks for you. You know when the shifts change. Finally, you exit, dawdle nearby the barracks, but you *don't* run in there, shooting and shooting and shooting. You wait till someone steps outside to get something or for a guard to take a piss. Then you shoot him.

If a Hummer full of guys comes zooming out of the gates—good. The IED your friends planted two weeks prior is wired and rearing to go a few blocks away. Maybe you'll get a half dozen of them that way.

Then back to the dark room. The water. The waiting. The wondering if anyone you know has been captured; whether they still retain their teeth, toes, or balls, and whether they told anyone where you are.

Is that a knock on the door? You have a shiv, and a gun with one bullet fewer than you did yesterday.

SAVE POINT.

Nick Mamatas is the author of *Under My Roof* (Soft Skull Press, 2006), a novel of nuclear proliferation for children, and the Bram Stoker and International Horror Guild Award-nominated Lovecraftian Beat road novel *Move Under Ground* (Night Shade Books, 2004). His short fiction has appeared in the *Mississippi Review*, *Razor*, *Spex*, *Polyphony*, and a dozen other venues, and his reportage and essays on radical politics have appeared in the *Village Voice*, *In These Times*, *Clamor*, and various anthologies by Disinformation Books. With Kap Su Seol he is the translator and co-author of *Kwangju Diary*, a study of urban insurrection in South Korea. A native New Yorker, Nick now lives near, but not in, Boston.

REFERENCES

Breznican, Anthony. "Army Recruiting Through Video Games." *Washington Post*, 23 May 2002.

Fielder, Joe. "GameSpot Review: *Halo*." *Game Spot* Online. Nov. 2001. <http://www.gamespot.com/Xbox/action/halo/review.html?page=1&q=&q=&q=9>.

Ignatius, David. "Think Strategy, Not Numbers." *Washington Post*, 26 Aug. 2003, sec. A13.

"Press Centre: US Armed Forces Invest $120m in Video Games." *Jane's Defence Weekly*. 13 Dec. 2005. <http://www.janes.com/press/articles/pc051213_1.shtml>.

Kemble, S. *Journals of Lieutenant-Colonel Stephen Kemble and British Army Orders 1775–1778*. New York: New York Historical Society, 1972.

Mao, Tse-tung. "The Strategy of Guerrilla Resistance Against Japan." *On Guerilla Warfare*. 20 Aug. 2006 (1937). <http://www.marxists.org/reference/archive/mao/works/1937/guerrilla-warfare/index.htm>.

Phill, Justin. "FAQ: *Halo* Combat Guide, Version 2.1." 2 Sept. 2004. *Game FAQs*. <http://db.gamefaqs.com/console/Xbox/file/halo_combat.txt>.

Schellong, Alexander. "*Defense News* Article." *Complexity and Social Networks Blog*. 15 May 2006. Institute for Quantitative Social Science and the Program on Networked Governance, Harvard University. <http://www.iq.harvard.edu/blog/netgov/2006/03/brinto_milward_on_dark_network.html>.

Schonauer, Scott. "Xbox Fever Hitting Europe Troops Hard": *Stars and Stripes_* (European edition), 7 July 2003.

Telzrow, M. E. "The 'Old Fox' Fools the Hounds: General George Washington, Referred to as the 'Old Fox' by Britain's Lord Cornwallis, Employed Innovative Measures to Outsmart the British and Win the Battle of Princeton." *The New American* 21 (26): 2005. 37–45.

Vox Day

HALO AND THE HIGH ART OF GAMES

A History of the First-Person Shooter

Why Halo *is like architecture, dance, poetry, and music…combined.*

IN 1849, THE GREAT COMPOSER Richard Wagner described what he considered to be the ideal artwork of the future, a holistic unification of the high arts he christened *Gesamtkunstwerk*. Wagner proposed this artistic vision as a "fire cure" for mankind, which would accomplish its miraculous effect by altering human sensibilities in the future from understanding to feeling. *Gestamtkunstwerk* was to be created by merging the distinct arts of music, poetry, and dance with architecture, sculpture, and painting, resulting in a revolutionary new form that would provide the audience with a sublime, purely emotional experience.

One hundred and forty-three years later, Wagner's vision of Total Art saw what may have been its first partial realization through four young men working together in Texas. Inspired by a classic Apple II game about a prisoner attempting to escape from a Nazi prison, John Carmack, John Romero, Tom Hall, and Adrian Carmack started id Software and produced *Wolfenstein 3D*, which was not intended as art but as pure entertainment for adrenaline junkies. While it might be stretching the metaphor to assert that *Wolfenstein 3D* incorporated poetry into the visceral violence it offered, the game definitely combined discern-able elements of music, architecture, sculpture, and painting in creating a sensual, emotional experience that was undeniably sublime.

And few who witnessed another individual attempting to escape from the ten levels of dreadful Nazi strongholds would attempt to argue that the art of dance was entirely absent. The non-stop, arrhythmic side-to-side motion of the player as he involuntarily mimicked the evasive motions of his on-screen avatar was a striking aspect of the game, one that bears testimony to the complete immersion of the player's consciousness in the virtual experience.

The power of that immersion is all the more impressive when one considers the crudity of the five Wagnerian elements involved in *Wolfenstein 3D*. While Bobby Prince's award-winning music was rivaled only by The Fat Man's within the game industry at the time, it consisted of nothing but twenty-two kilohertz synthesized electronics piped through an 8-bit Soundblaster. The architecture was a simplistic Bauhaus interpretation of a lab-rat's maze, the sculpture was not only cartoonish but was not even truly three-dimensional, and the painting was limited by the low-resolution VGA graphics and a palette of only 256 colors.[1]

Neither the storyline nor the characters were exactly what one would describe as complex. If B. J. Blazkowicz's motivation of escaping from a Nazi prison was not hard to understand, the motivations of his antagonists, Hans Grosse, the evil Dr. Schabbs, and robo-Hitler, remain a mystery. And yet, the whole was greater than the sum of the parts, for if the emotions inspired by the game were less lofty than those invoked by the Ring Cycle, they were arguably more powerful. While I have seen men and women cry at the opera, I have never heard more piercing screams than from an audience of one caught up in watching a session of *Wolfenstein 3D*.[2]

But although it was the first great step toward *Gesamtkunstwerk* and brought the now-popular genre of the 3D action game into the public consciousness, *Wolfenstein 3D* was not the original first-person shooter. That honor belongs to a game called *Spasim*, which dates back to 1974 and is remarkable not only for its early use of a first-person perspective and 3D wireframe graphics, but also for its incorporation of worldwide

---

[1] Two hundred and fifty-five, actually; hot pink had to be reserved for transparencies.

[2] I must confess that I nearly wet myself while playing *Wolfenstein 3D* one evening, although that was mostly because the audience's scream was right in my left ear.

online multiplayer action. Like *Maze War*, a rival claimant for the title of first first-person shooter, *Spasim* ran on mainframe computers and was mostly played at universities.

Star Raiders, which ran on the Atari 400 computer, appeared in 1979 and was the first of many space combat games. Its use of wireframe graphics and true 3D makes it worthy of note, but of far more ultimate importance to the genre was Richard Garriott's *Akalabeth: World of Doom*, which was written for the Apple II in BASIC and distributed in plastic bags by Garriott himself in 1980 prior to California Pacific's decision to pick up the publishing rights.

Akalabeth was the first computer game I remember playing, and although its black-and-white graphics were primitive stick figures and its screen refreshes were measured in seconds per frame instead of frames per second, it was nevertheless as absorbing and as exciting in its own way as the *Dungeons & Dragons* role-playing game it was designed to mimic. Despite its first-person perspective and its obvious visual relationship to *Wolfenstein 3D* and subsequent first-person shooters, *Akalabeth* is not often cited as a genre precursor, mostly because of its massive role in another gaming genre, namely, that of the role-playing game.

For if its graphics foreshadowed the shooter, the game itself was the direct ancestor of one of the great game series of all time, namely, *Ultima*. In fact, *Akalabeth* is unofficially known as *Ultima 0*, and Richard Garriott may be better known as the persona in which he appears in the Ultima games, Lord British. While the first-person perspective remained in the dungeon-crawling portions of many subsequent Ultima games and in every later RPG from Wizardry series to the Daggerfall line, the focus of the gameplay never revolved around the perspective, which is why the genre to which *Wolfenstein 3D* and *Halo* belong requires being delineated as a first-person "shooter" or a 3D "action" game.

But the importance of *Akalabeth* to the first-person shooter genre does not end with its graphical perspective. For in 1987, Origin Systems, the very successful company that Richard Garriott founded to produce *Ultimas III* through *IX*, (to say nothing of *Autoduel*, the *Ultima Underworlds*, and the *Wing Commander* series), hired a twenty-year-old programmer named John Romero to port Apple II games to the Commodore 64.

But if *Wolfenstein* made id's two Johns, Romero and Carmack, successful, it was *Doom* that made them notorious and confirmed that the first-person shooter was a *bona fide* gaming genre in its own right. Whereas the incorporation of fear had been largely incidental to the design in *Wolf*, it was an overt and intentional element of *Doom* from its moment of conception. From its ominous strings to the elements of madness in the storyline, from the terrifying appearance of the oversized monsters to the ghastly chainsaw-and-bazooka butchery in which the player is forced to engage, *Doom* was an awesome and overwhelming experience that didn't so much leave an emotional impression on the player as an intense psychic beating.

Doom inspired a host of imitators based on similar 2.5D technology, collectively known as *Doom*-clones. Unfortunately, too many publishers and game designers failed to understand that what made *Doom* such a visceral and absorbing experience was the way in which it provoked an emotional reaction from the player. The abrupt shift from silence and darkness, interrupted only by eerie strings and guttural breathing, to the roar of a saw carving through hordes of shrieking, flame-throwing demons, could leave a player fired up and unable to sleep for hours after turning off the computer. These lesser game makers failed to see the art; they saw only the blood.

These *Doom*-clones ranged from the good (*Heretic* and *Star Wars: Dark Forces*) to the bad (*Chex Quest, Witchhaven, TekWar*), the ugly (*Rise of the Triad, Redneck Rampage*), and the obscure (*CyClones*,[3] *Rebel Moon, Powerslave*). GT Interactive, which acquired the publishing rights to *Doom II* and published more *Doom*-clones than one can count on both hands, even went so far as to publish a game titled, quite simply, *Blood*.[4]

Each clone attempted to add something new to the basic game concept or at least put a different shine to it in order to capture a share of *Doom's* massive market. *Heretic, HeXen,* and *Witchhaven* made use of fantasy settings, *Dark Forces* allowed the player to enter the Star Wars universe, *Rise of the Triad* introduced environmental modification and jump pads, *Rebel Moon Rising*[5] experimented with speech recognition, and *TekWar* paid testimony to the fact that William Shatner's name did not sell games as effectively as books.

The two most successful clones were *Duke Nukem 3D* and *Deer Hunt-*

---

[3] Full disclosure: Paul Sebastien and I did the music and sound effects for this SSI game.

[4] Contrary to what its name implies, *Blood* was more than a mere gore-fest and was better than the average *Doom*-clone. *Blood II*, on the other hand, blew.

[5] Full disclosure: I designed and co-produced *Rebel Moon* and *Rebel Moon Rising*. Few people have heard of them since they were primarily marketed through bundling with Creative Labs and Intel hardware. *Rebel Moon Rising* was published by GT Interactive, but speech recognition turned out to be of little appeal to the gaming world at that time.

er. *Duke Nukem* combined humor with excellent gameplay and caused more gamers to quote the movie *They Live* than have ever seen it or even heard of it.[6] It was also controversial for its inclusion of gyrating strippers and generally more adult themes than had been seen before in computer games not designed primarily as pixilated soft porn. But for all of *Duke Nukem's* success, *Deer Hunter* was arguably the more important game, as despite its outdated technology and simplistic gameplay,[7] it created the sub-genre of the hunting game and introduced millions of non-gamers to computer gaming while simultaneously opening up a new software distribution channel through mainstream retailers such as Wal-Mart, Target, and even Cabela's.

While the rest of the industry was moving to catch up to id Software, however, id was raising the bar even higher. In 1996, Carmack and Romero introduced *Quake*, which was rather dark, ugly, and muddy in comparison with the brightly colored *Doom* and its clones, but introduced true 3D graphics[8] to the genre. The move to 3D was not as revolutionary as it appears, since a number of 3D games outside the first-person shooter genre had already been produced,[9] but it was significant since it drove the hardware manufacturers to supply the 3D acceleration hardware needed for the tremendous amount of mathematical computations required by the new 3D gaming engines.

Few development houses and even fewer publishers were prepared to blow off nearly every computer in existence by setting minimum system requirements higher than anything being shipped by the computer manufacturers, but John Carmack was, and is, a performance junkie, and with three massive hits under id's belt, no one was about to tell him that what he wanted to do was unreasonable. Indeed, even mainstream giants such as Intel and Microsoft were willing to cater to Carmack, knowing that in feeding the voracious appetite of performance-hungry gamers they were generating the need for a new generation of hardware.

And *Quake* was a huge success, although not primarily because of

---

[6] "It's time to kick ass and chew bubble gum, and I'm all outta gum."

[7] Or, as a friend of mine who is now an executive at THQ insists, *because* of its simplistic gameplay.

[8] This is not true 3D in the tactile sense or even the 1950s movie sense, but since I am one of the few owners of a true 3D gaming system—Nintendo's Virtual Boy—I feel quite justified using the term in this colloquial sense.

[9] Some industry observers include *Descent* in the list of *Doom* clones. Given that it was a true 3D engine versus *Doom's* 2.5D, its vastly different gameplay, and the fact that it requires an entirely different game controller, this is absurd.

its disturbing 3D environments or its Internet gameplay, but because of Carmack's brilliant decision to open up significant aspects of the game to would-be designers. This allowed players to not only modify their characters and create their own 3D environments, but to actually create different games within the game, such as team capture the flag. If *Quake* did not offer much in the way of single-player innovation, it nevertheless represents an important point of departure in the first-person shooter between games designed in the traditional manner for a single human player and those designed with multiplayer action in mind. Indeed, *Quake III: Arena*, *Starsiege: Tribes*, *Unreal Tournament*, and *Wolfenstein: Enemy Territory* don't even offer an option for solo play.

The game industry, like many industries, is remarkably small when seen from the inside. Although it has grown dramatically over the last decade, there are those who still remember when Chris Crawford held the first Computer Game Developer's Conference in his living room in 1987.[10] One result, presumably unforeseen by John Carmack or anyone else was the way in which *Quake's* open architecture would open the way for new talent to enter the industry.

The ability to experiment with *Quake* inspired many would-be game designers. In one case of particular note, two Microsoft employees had worked there long enough to amass the resources necessary to acquire a license to the *Quake* engine. Unlike the many *Doom*-licensees of a generation before, however, Gabe Newell and Mike Harrington were not content to simply churn out another *Quake* clone, but instead made clever use of scripted sequences and in-game cinematics, thus turning what had previously been a series of distinct levels into a continuous, plot-driven narrative.

Half-Life was hugely successful. But it was not the only popular post-*Quake* first-person shooter. The gaming world had been waiting for *Unreal* for years, ever since Epic announced it by showing off an extremely misleading series of beautiful screenshots that could never possibly have run on the unaccelerated computer system it claimed was the minimum system required. But after a delay of almost two years,[11] *Unreal* was fi-

---

[10] I still mourn CGDC's move from the Westin. How can you not miss the Origin guys picking up those $750 tabs at the bar?

[11] I was at the GT Interactive party where Dante Anderson, who was also the executive producer of *Rebel Moon Revolution*, was publicly thanked in front of the entire crowd by a very grateful Ron Chaimowitz for finally getting the *Unreal* team to finish its long-awaited project. I have never seen a roomful of people go silent faster, nor laugh louder, than when Dante took the mike from Ron and said: "I guess there will never be a better time to tell you I spent $11,000 taking the team out to a strip club to celebrate going gold."

nally completed in time for the E3 show in 1998, and, unlike most long-delayed games, it proved worthy of the wait.

Bad and belated translations of the most popular games to consoles notwithstanding, first-person shooters were almost exclusively developed for PCs because of their greater video memory and ability to make use of special 3D acceleration cards. But finally, with the release of the sixth-generation of video consoles that contained the same sort of 3D acceleration chips around which the PC cards were built, it became possible for video gamers to enjoy the fast first-person shooter action that had hitherto required a much more expensive computer.

While the Sega Dreamcast was more known for fighting games such as *Soul Calibur* and strange translations of unusual Japanese games, *GoldenEye 007* became a major hit on the Nintendo 64.[12] Although it preceded both *Half-Life* and *Thief: The Dark Project*, *GoldenEye* made use of its James Bond storyline and stealthy tactics in a manner reminiscent of both of these popular PC games. It also offered surprisingly good multiplayer action. Although a sequel was produced, *GoldenEye: Rogue Agent* (another first-person shooter from the same development team), *Perfect Dark* saw more success.

Sony's PS2, being the most popular of the three systems, naturally saw a plethora of first-person shooters produced for it or ported to it. However, the games most popular on the PlayStation have been military-related shooters, especially those dealing with World War II. While GT Interactive's *Nam* was an early, PC-based military shooter, the sub-genre really took off with *Tom Clancy's Ghost Recon* series. That modern combat game was followed by other shooters such as *Medal of Honor*, *Battlefield 1942*, and *Call of Duty*, all of which are set in various WWII theatres. These military shooters tend to be even more heavily scripted than *Half-Life* and feature fewer puzzles and a much more realistic appearance than most first-person shooters.

At this point, it is perhaps worth noting that despite its importance in the early days of gaming, the name of Apple has hardly appeared since the early 1980s. Despite the significance of the Apple II to many of the game industry's most important figures, Apple ceased to be relevant once VGA and 320x200, 256 color graphics became available on the IBM PC.

---

[12] The Nintendo 64 is actually considered to be a fifth-generation system, but no major first-person shooters were produced for the sixth-generation Nintendo GameCube.

Despite the Macintosh's graphical operating system and technological superiority, Apple's problematic relationship with third-party vendors and its relative lack of mass popularity meant that game developers had little incentive to write software for the Macintosh. Thus, most Mac games were either amateurish ripoffs of more popular PC games or outdated ports of games that had been popular some years before.

But every niche finds someone to fill it in the end. A little company that got its start in the game industry by producing a freeware Pong-clone called *Gnop!* then, in 1993, produced the first Macintosh FPS, called *Pathways Into Darkness*, which was a rather unattractive little game that looked rather like a cross between *Ultima Underworld* and Mitch Albom's *Five People You Meet In Heaven*. Bungie followed that up with *Marathon*, which was known as "*Doom* for the Mac" and, as is customary in Macintosh cult circles, was widely asserted to be much better than *Doom* despite the fact that neither it nor its sequel, *Durandal and Infinity*, even featured modem network play, or any gameplay elements that approached id's ghastly genius.

Bungie publicly announced *Halo: Combat Evolved* at the 1999 Macworld Expo, but the acquisition of the company by Microsoft less than a year later meant that the game would be released on Microsoft's new Xbox console instead of for the Mac OS. This was a major coup for Microsoft and may have even saved the Xbox from an embarrassing failure, as with the exception of *Dead or Alive 3*, a fighting game franchise most notable for lavish attention paid to the large and wobbly breasts of its female characters, there were no significant games that required an Xbox to play them.

Every new console needs its killer game in order to survive, and fortunately for Microsoft, *Halo* proved to be that game. *Halo* followed *Half-Life*'s lead in moving away from the concept of static, puzzle-based levels, which tended to reduce gameplay to a simple matter of finding a key to unlock the final door, as its use of more realistic SF environments allowed the gamer to enter more fully into the game's universe. In this, Bungie was likely aided by its experience in developing strategy games, as the 3D outside environments of *Myth* inspired its designers to think beyond the dungeon-crawl mentality that had been a feature of the genre since *Akalabeth*.

The ability to climb into vehicles and make use of them only made the experience richer and more compelling, but perhaps even more impressive was *Halo's* ability to overcome the limitations of the Xbox controller. Prior to *Halo*, the ports of first-person shooters from PCs to video game consoles had been very disappointing, and the lack of a mouse made the situation even more problematic. Compounding this was the Xbox's dreadful game controller,[13] which was almost completely unsuited for human hands.

Nevertheless, *Halo's* designers managed to overcome this triple challenge and triggered an onslaught of console-based first-person shooters that shows no signs of stopping anytime soon. And yet, despite its success both in terms of gameplay innovation and market success, its most lasting legacy may well be an artistic one. For in 2003, a small group of inebriated game reviewers in Texas created what was intended to be a little parody movie by recording gameplay and using *Halo's* first-person view as camera. This eventually turned into *Red vs. Blue: The Blood Gulch Chronicles*, an ongoing machinima series that now has four seasons available on DVD.

And while games and their machinimatic offspring are still currently well below the radar of the arts community, it is worth noting that there is no other medium that is so well-suited for the expression of Wagner's *Gesamtkunstwerk*. There is no shortage of music in the genre; *Halo* even won a "best original soundtrack" from *Rolling Stone* magazine, and award-winning composers such as John Williams[14] have been writing music for computer games for more than a decade now.

3D environments are no longer limited to first-person shooters, of course; the popularity of the games has driven computer manufacturers to build 3D acceleration right onto the motherboard of most machines sold today, and one can visit real cities from Chicago to Rome in various games, to say nothing of fictional places such as Vice City. These environments not only incorporate architecture, but many of them are actually built by trained architects, using the same software used to design buildings in the real world.

The same technology is used for the characters who inhabit these worlds, a virtual sculpture that shapes true three-dimensional objects from pixels that can then be used for solid freeform fabrication to create actual physical sculptures. Painting, being a mere two-dimensional art,

---

[13] Apparently inspired by the oversized controller of the Atari Jaguar, a failed 64-bit system, Microsoft's original Xbox controller was a clunky nightmare. I own nearly every video game system, from Atari Pong to the Vectrex, but I put off buying an Xbox until they came out with a new controller.

[14] Star Wars.

is simple and has been an integral part of gaming since programmers realized that machines were fast enough to push more than their blocky, homemade pixel-art and began hiring genuine artists.

It is true that neither poetry nor dance figure prominently in any games yet produced, but the technology is already there to support both. The development of synthetic speech technology means that even the longest poem need not be pre-recorded as canned wave samples, and even allows for the use of poems generated by in-game artificial intelligences. The possibilities for dance are even more obvious, as motion capture technology is now sophisticated enough to record and replay the most challenging ballet movements; it is only the fact that the gaming world is almost completely divorced from the world of the cultural arts that has prevented these possibilities from hitherto being realized.

The imaginative observer may even ascertain unique aspects of *Gesamtkunstwerk* in *Halo* proper. At the very beginning of the game, the player is drawn to participate in a ballet of sorts, as the militarily improbable firefight on the beach owes as much to dance as it does to modern projectile combat. The open environment with its mountain-ringed bowl open to the sky takes on an aspect of a stage, albeit one without an audience, as the player alternately bounds forward and leaps from side to side as he attempts to keep pace with the rest of his troop.

And *Halo*'s use of reusable environments in the place of idiosyncratic puzzle-driven levels brings architecture to the fore, as it is used for three purposes: to establish a sense of place, to tell a piece of the storyline in a visual format, and to provide a physical platform for the gameplay experience. In this, the game's architecture is asked to fulfill a role similar to that played by the cathedrals of the medieval period, buildings that were expected to tell a story as well as serve a purpose. That the architecture of *Halo* is more ethereal than that of the cathedral and that it serves more mundane ends does not lessen the similarity of the usage. Indeed, there are devotees of pure materialism who might reasonably insist that the game's ultimate object of temporal amusement is more concrete than the cathedral's purposeful glorification of a trans-temporal sky deity.[15]

It is only in its attempt to provide a richer storyline that *Halo*'s designers consciously attempt to fulfill an important artistic aspect of Total Art

---

[15] Being a worshipper of said sky deity myself, I do not make this argument, I merely admit to its theoretically rational basis.

that is nevertheless not one of the six primary *Gesamtkunstwerkgrund-heiten.*[16] In this, I would argue that they were not entirely successful, but unlike *Doom*, *Quake*, or *Half-Life*, they were successful enough to create what promises to be an ongoing story, and one that will, like the Ring Cycle, surely spawn offshoots providing a wide variety of experiences.

While the world may pray it never sees abominations such as *Quake: Swan Lake* or *Nutcracker 3D: Triumph of the Mouse King*, the fact remains that first-person shooters such as *Halo* prove that Wagner's vision of Total Art is technologically feasible at last. It is impossible to say who will be the first genius to identify himself as a Total Artist and create a holistic work worthy of being proclaimed a *Gesamtkunstwerk*, but his appearance is all but inevitable now that the technological groundwork has been completed. The palm leaves are strewn, the ass awaits, and only the identity of this first New Wagnerian and the nature of his creation remains to be revealed to Mankind.

> **Vox Day** is a novelist and game designer. As to the inevitable question of what he was drinking when he wrote this, the answer is Amaretto.

---

[16] "Elements of Total Art." The best thing about German is that it's perfectly acceptable to make up your own words. The longer, of course, the better.

Daniel Barbour

343 Guilty Spark:

The floating blue orb better known as "343 Guilty Spark" is the AI Monitor, caretaker, and historian who was apparently left to keep watch over Alpha Halo Installation 04 and its contents when the Forerunner departed. Like most human AIs, 343 has several behavioral blocks in place—for example, he cannot retrieve the Index from the Library or reunite it with the Core. He needs the Master Chief, Mobuto, Miranda Keyes, Sgt. Johnson, or another being fitting the description and criteria of "Reclaimer" (seemingly any member of the Human race) to do this for him.

343 is quirky and good-humored, though at the same time detached, and one who operates by the book. Protocol is king; the slight emotion shown for those who die along the way is fleeting; he seems only to truly mourn the simple inconvenience of finding yet another to assist him. "Having had considerable time" to check and re-check the systems of Halo in his masters' absence, it is quite likely that his isolation has given more than a slight opportunity for an unusual melancholy, egotism, or instability (call it what you will) to bubble to the surface.

Freed from his commitments on Installation 04 with its destruction, the Monitor was happily retrieved by a group of "Heretics": an Elite and his followers preaching open rebellion against the Prophets and their lies of the supposed salvation the Great Journey has to offer. With the slaying of the Heretic leader, 343 (reverently referred to by the Covenant as "The Oracle") was summarily captured and interrogated by the Prophets before eventually falling in alongside the newly united forces of the Arbiter, Miranda Keyes, and Sgt. Johnson. Now, if everyone could just stop fighting long enough to hear what he's got to say.

2401 Penitent Tangent:

2401 Penitent Tangent is the red-tinged Monitor/AI left by the Forerunner with the similar charge of maintaining Delta Halo 05. Little is known about him or how long he had been in the custody of Gravemind when first introduced, but he appears to be no less concerned with a strict adherence to protocol. Although, after all these years, he seems to be a tad less worse for wear emotionally than 343. His present situation is unknown.

The Arbiter:

In times of crisis, an Elite warrior is chosen to don the ancient armor and assume the role of the Arbiter: "The Will of the Prophets." The nature of the Arbiter's challenges (to quell threats and insurrections) guarantee his death, but also his internment in the hallowed Mausoleum to sleep with the Blessed who have gone before.

And so, the Fleet Commander of the Covenant Armada "Particular Justice" at Halo 04 was condemned to death for heresy, having failed at his charge and allowing the Sacred Ring to be destroyed. His appeals on the grounds of the unpredictable nature of "The Demon" (the Master Chief) and of the struggles encountered with the release of the parasite (The Flood) were ignored. Following his public torture, he was brought before the Prophets of Truth and Mercy and allowed the chance to redeem himself in concert with his execution. He would become the Arbiter in order to quell a band of Heretics, but he would surely die in the process; the Council would have their corpse. And yet, he has survived time and time again.

Following the betrayal of the Elites, the Arbiter remained in shock and disbelief that the Prophets would turn on them—their co-founders in the Covenant—and that the Great Journey was, in truth, a lie. Even his introduction to the Master Chief in the presence of Gravemind was not enough. But, as he continued his quest for revenge, the pieces slowly drifted into place. In the end, only an (hopefully symbolic) alliance with Johnson and Miranda allowed him the opportunity both to "stop the key from turning" and, at least partially, avenge his murdered brethren.

The Ark:

The dominion of the Forerunner was vast indeed. Artifacts and installations of countless worlds lie buried, for the most part untainted by the passage of time. Stones and relics found at most of the sites contain coordinates leading to others. Many of the human colony worlds were accidentally located by the Covenant this way—Reach and Earth being the most recent examples. They were also used to find Halo 04 by Humans and Covenant alike, and from some relic on Earth (though the primary facility seems to have remained undiscovered), regret appears to have found his way to Halo 05. The Halos, the seven rings left in their perpetual orbits after activation, and the subsequent destruction of their creators, are nothing short of astounding. But, as revealed by 343 Guilty Spark, there remains yet another installation more grand and more pivotal, than any yet seen.

Hypothesized and speculated on for some time, but only revealed in *Halo 2*'s conclusion (and the *Halo 3* announcement trailer), the Ark is still shrouded in mystery. Located on Earth, buried beneath the plains of eastern Africa, the Ark is a kilometers-wide, primary station (fortress? shelter?) from which the entire Halo network may be activated remotely. It is not known whether the Ark will completely preserve the lives (or the way of life) of those who set it off (unlike the Halos, which destroy even the sentient life upon their surfaces), but the name, a biblical allusion to a place of sanctuary during a storm, implies that it will.

That some members of Humanity (namely ONI) previously knew of this installation (and others less magnificent) is certain. For how long, and to what ends, they have used this knowledge is uncertain.

Does the specific location of the Ark have anything to do with the Prophets' mad zeal to annihilate Mankind? What does it mean that Humanity occupies the world of the Ark, possibly the last haven of the

Forerunner in this galaxy? Is this yet another clue as to why 343 seems content to call every Human a "Reclaimer," yet not a Forerunner? Is it mere coincidence, or should Humanity refer to the Forerunner as *father*, *former master*, or *once ally*?

Cortana:

Cortana is one of hundreds (thousands?) of AIs that populate the computer networks of the Human worlds. The production of an AI is an intensive process; they do not come cheap and are reserved for the most exclusive and demanding tasks. Above and beyond this, however, Cortana is unique: as a Class-III AI, she is a direct copy of a human being, Dr. Halsey (or at least of the flash-cloned mind destroyed in the transcribing process). Lacking behavioral inhibitors of any kind (and able to override those that may happen to inconveniently arise), she is both free and creative. Unlike most other military AIs (such as the ONI AI Beowulf), which are strict, sullen, and methodical, Cortana, on the other hand, is strong-headed, noisy, and somewhat off-the-wall.

However, her freedom comes at a price. As a "smart" AI, she has an unextendable life-span of approximately seven years, at which time she will become simply too intelligent, suffering from an "exponential attenuation of function"; in other words, she will inevitably think so much she will forget to breathe.

At her choosing, she and the Master Chief were specifically paired together for MJOLNIR Mark V/SPARTAN-II proving trials in preparation for her placement aboard the *Pillar of Autumn* for its covert infiltration mission to capture and return with a ruling member of the Covenant hegemony to force negotiations. The mission was unfortunately cut short by the Covenant invasion of the mission's launch point, Reach, and Cortana's blind (though not uncalculated) jump to the system of Halo 04. In the midst of the *Pillar of Autumn's* fiery descent to Halo, her safety (as well as that of the UNSC coordinate data she possessed) could be assured in only one place—the suit of the Master Chief.

However, since her time in Halo 04's Control Center, Cortana has found herself laden with vast amounts of hastily compressed data, the review of which would surely initiate consequences beyond anyone's wildest expectations. There simply has not been a chance or location to thoroughly unload or analyze it, something that has frustrated her to no end. The fate of this priceless data (no doubt seized in part by ONI upon the pair's return to Earth) is unknown.

In spite of this, her "spare" time has already allowed her to exceed the Covenant's knowledge of their own technology, refining their cumbersome (though already undeniably effective) cudgels in order to create focused streams of energy, a Slipspace system capable of jumps much closer to gravity wells (even directly over planetary settlements...), and enabling her to make copies of herself: all further proof of the Covenant's lack of comprehension of, and holy reliance on, their stolen ordnance, and also allowing her to wreak even greater havoc during fleet engagements.

While the speed and remorselessness with which she may willfully circumvent her own ethical protocols is chilling (simply venting the atmosphere of a desired enemy ship to "remove" the crew), the events involved in Earth's initial defense and at Delta Halo 05 left little doubt of her continuing dedication to the survival of the Human race. Perhaps it is this veneer of loyalty that makes her meeting with Gravemind all the more disheartening. He has many questions, and Cortana seems all too willing to answer them.

The Covenant:

The Covenant is a religious alliance initially founded between the Elites (Sangheili) and the Prophets (native name unknown). Once at war with one another, their joint discovery of Forerunner technology solidified a union whereby the Elites would provide protection as the Prophets searched for the means by which the "God-like" Forerunner had transcended reality and found their "salvation." (The exact nature of, and the beliefs surrounding, the Covenant's [upper-case] Gods is unknown.) On the way, they have converted (read: subjugated) at least seven, though possibly more, species. These races include, but may or may not be limited to: the diminutive Grunts (Unggoy), the bird-like Jackals (Kig-yar), the insectoid Drones (Yanme'e), the armored, worm-like composite beasts known as Hunters (Lekgolo), the ape-like Brutes (Jiralhanae), the buoyant Engineers (Huragok; from the novels), and the hulking Drinol Beasts (possibly called the Sharquoi; seen only in concept art).

The Covenant has a relatively high level of technology, mainly accrued from excavated Forerunner installations. The seat of their power, and the only homeworld they seem to have, is the planetoid *High Charity*—a tremendous semi-spherical habitat and battle-station dozens of kilometers across, powered at its center by an actual Forerunner vessel. Most of their weapons are referred to as "plasma" based (though their actual nature and mechanisms are not clearly understood), with the exception of the fuel-rod, particle beam, and needle ordnance. Their starships are much faster than Human vessels and are capable of pinpoint maneuvering while in FTL travel, as is made explicitly clear several times in the novel *The Fall of Reach* when Covenant ships materialize right in the center of Human battlegroups. Their technological feats seem coupled with what can only be described as a reverent ignorance; they seem unable, unwilling, and vehemently against any attempts (by Covenant or Human agents) to improve upon any Forerunner relics they come to acquire. To do so would be blasphemy.

This alliance, however, is far from secure. The Covenant ranks have been rife with unrest and even assassinations within recent years. With the exception of the two founding races (and the further exception of the mercenary Jackals), all others have joined the Covenant through force and now exist as part of a caste system with strict rules guiding their upbringing and socialization, in an attempt to prevent any true unity among the conquered peoples. In the times of trouble and insurrection that have inevitably occurred, a chosen Elite has risen to become the Arbiter and reestablished the so-called peace.

Though the Covenant's hatred for those filthy primates called Humans is both harsh and powerful, there remains some confusion over the precise transgression the Human race has inflicted against the Gods. The details of this Holy War appear to be known only to the Prophets; there is confusion among the Elites as to why the Humans, having proven their tenacity and worth in battle countless times, have not been offered the sanctuary of the Covenant alongside the others. From where this hatred springs, how it relates to the Covenant's "Great Journey," and, more importantly, how Man may manage to survive them both, has yet to be discovered.

The Halos, according to Cortana and the Covenant databanks, hold a deep religious power over the Covenant. They have searched for these seven rings for some time, and it is through them, they believe, that their Great Journey is to be accomplished. Needless to say, they are profoundly important to them, so much so that they avoid firing upon the *Pillar of Autumn* for risk of striking one. Upon the Humans' arrival at Halo 04, the Covenant was already on the ring's surface, following course and scouring the ring for technology they could wield for their own purposes. An oddity is their "discovery" of the Flood. They were discovered and "released" (whether intentionally or not is unknown) by the Covenant—Human tinkering merely made the problem worse. However, while terrifying, the Flood is not entirely unexpected to the Covenant. It seems that they have encountered the Flood before and may have quite a history with them.

Spurned by the heresy of Halo 04's destruction, the Covenant juggernaut resumed its search for the other rings and installations, unwittingly stumbling upon Earth in the process. Not knowing that it was the Human homeworld but only that it contained some Forerunner relic, the small fleet led by the impetuous Prophet of Regret was repelled relatively easily, but not before a distress signal could be sent to the rest of the armada(s). By following in the wake of Regret's retreat, yet another ring was discovered, and it became apparent that the Great Journey so desperately sought by the Covenant Hierarchs was nothing more than the activation of the Halo network; their Journey would not bring salvation, only death.

As these events unfolded, the ignorant ambition of the Brutes, coupled with some shadowy need of the Prophets to remove the Elites, spilled over into bloodshed. What began with the replacement of the Elite Honor Guard with Brute personnel under mysterious circumstances ended with the murder of the Elite Council members and total civil war. Sides have been drawn, with the religiously disillusioned Elites, Grunts, and Hunters at odds against the Prophets, Brutes, Jackals, and Drones.

Whether this conflict will benefit Humanity as they continue to struggle against the still overwhelming Covenant presence (and occupation) on Earth remains to be seen.

Covenant Civil War:

They were once bitter enemies, and neither theology nor common goal has ever been enough to instill perfect trust between the Elites and the Prophets. As a military giant scouring the galaxy for technology often buried on already occupied worlds, attacking and eventually assimilating various encountered races is nothing new. However, the Prophets' relentless campaign to hunt Humanity to extinction has begun to raise eyebrows among even some of the most dedicated Elite warriors. It is apparent that the details of Humanity's transgressions against the Gods, other than that they are an abomination (and that they have somehow, somewhere "blocked access to sacred sites"), are not truly known to those outside of the Hierarchs' caucus.

This uneasiness between the Elites and Prophets reached a flashpoint with the recent assimilation of the powerful and ambitious Brute race into the Covenant. The Brutes are mere pawns; while they despise the Elites out of simple jealousy and competitiveness, the Prophets, specifically Truth, seem all too willing to use this adversity to further some hidden agenda, some buried grudge, manifested thus far with the demotion and eventual expulsion of the Elites from the Covenant. Both steps took place under questionable circumstances. That Truth both recalled countless Covenant ships inbound on the Master Chief, thereby facilitating and assuring Regret's assassination, and also "let [Mercy] go" when he was attacked by a Flood Infection form implies yet another level of deceit within the Hierarchy. It also raises further questions of Truth's true motivations and just how much he has personally orchestrated not only the war on the Human race or the Elite betrayal, but other important events without the knowledge of even the other ruling Prophets. It remains to be seen whether his selfishness springs from some secret knowledge of the Forerunner (i.e., perhaps he does not truly believe in the Covenant religion at all) or from boundless zeal as he attempts to achieve "salvation" with as few to share it with as possible.

The Flood:

A species so eminently threatening that a powerful and ancient civilization constructed habitable rings 10,000 kilometers in diameter to contain and observe them. The Flood are as numerous as they are voracious; they neither surrender nor retreat. The Flood appear to be both sentient and omni-parasitic—preying upon any host utilizing a certain minimum level of sentience and bio-mass—and can infiltrate "even advanced life forms." It is not known whether they were merely encountered or created by the Forerunner for some purpose known only, as of yet, to themselves.

There are five known types of Flood. There is the Ranger/Infection class, the Carrier/Incubator class, a Worker/Soldier class, a Command/Pilot form (seen from the growth infecting ships and structures), and the Gravemind intelligence (including its preliminary stages of development, such as that which enveloped Captain Keyes). To explain how the process begins would lead into a chicken-and-the-egg discussion, so we will begin at the Infection form.

The Infection forms are small, tentacled creatures that have their own defined biological framework and that are not dependent upon a host. An Infection form will seek out any life-form of necessary bio-mass and calcium deposits to sustain itself and proceed to attempt to use the creature as a host in a sequence of actions: tapping into the spinal system, suppressing the host's consciousness, embedding itself in the thoracic cavity, and causing the host to mutate. (343 Guilty Spark mentions "spores" during his own synopsis of the Flood life-cycle, which may simply be another term for the Infection form, or perhaps an even more base form of the Flood.) From here, it is assumed that one of three changes will occur in the host.

The first is that the host will remain *relatively* physically unchanged (if you consider "relatively unchanged" to include tentacle growth, organ rearrangement, necrosis, and eventual consumption), save for the Infection form embedded in it. These would be the Worker/Soldier class, used for manual labor such as building, gathering, repairing, or defensive/offensive actions. So far, only Marines and Elites have been seen to mutate into Workers/Soldiers. (It is unknown whether the ominous "Juggernaut" form hidden on the *Halo 2* disc is a Worker/Soldier of another race, or yet another form entirely.)

The second host possibility is that of the Carrier, which presumably only affects creatures who are physically or mentally unsuitable to be Workers/Soldiers (such as Grunts or Jackals). The Carriers grow large epidermic sacs that contain several Infection-class Flood. When a Carrier is in close proximity to any number of suitable hosts, it triggers some manner of biochemical reaction, causing the pus-filled sacs to explode and spread the smaller forms in order to infect more hosts and perpetuate the cycle of reproduction. When the Flood's inability (unwillingness) to suitably care for the integrity of the host body has caused sufficient degeneration, the Worker/Soldier class will also change into the Carrier form.

The conglomerate stages of the Flood have been encountered only rarely and studied even less. Therefore, the processes of their creation and growth remain uncertain. Found on the bridge of the *Truth and Reconciliation*, one such large, multi-appendaged amalgamation appears to be a combined symbiosis including several, at least in this case, Human hosts. Other than extracting information, its capabilities and roles are unknown. On High Charity, other such growths are seen lining the walls and apparently even piloting Pelican dropships (the conjectured Pilot or Command form), though this time with no obvious hosts involved.

How these forms fit into the development and nature of the central-consciousness, the Gravemind, taunts us all the more.

Though they appear to have a relatively simple procedure for reproduction, as 343 Guilty Spark states, the "parasitic nature of the Flood belies their intelligence." What is interesting is that they are able to function (even assimilate) the machinery and technology of their host to an amazing degree and are able to fire weaponry and repair damaged electrical and mechanical equipment at a surprisingly nominal level. They have (as we learn through Keyes) the ability to access host memory, strip it from them piece by piece, and utilize it to their advantage; the lesser Flood also possess some semblance of this ability, though from what we have seen, they do not appear to have such a pronounced sense of self; they do not exert the same levels of mental force or operate nearly as methodically.

And although the Halo network is meant to ultimately starve and contain the Flood, their continued existence after a previous firing and eons of isolation shows ever more that though they may be restricted and slowed, as a whole they are not so easily destroyed. The hunger of the Flood seems limitless, yet they fear the starvation and slumber that an exhaustion of their food supply would bring; something that has happened once before with the Halos' firing and, curiously, would also inevitably happen again if the Flood had their way and consumed all in their path. Perhaps with the Gravemind's rationality comes the ability to compromise.

Forerunner:

A contemplative mind seemingly content with its slight understanding of the Forerunner will not long be left ungnawed by the cankering tooth of mystery. Although their cyclopean architecture still remains, they have long been absent from their own creations. What little we know of them is explained vicariously through their machinery and their automatons. Clearly, they were technologically superior to both Humanity and the Covenant. Their influence (empire?) spanned at least this galaxy, encompassing both Einsteinian reality and Slipspace. They are not the Covenant's gods but are revered as God-like, having supposedly found the path to salvation.

At one point in the Forerunners' history, they encountered the Flood. They fought and retreated. When they had at last exhausted every tactical option, the Halo network was activated; as far as 343 Guilty Spark's data shows, they, and all other sentient life capable of supporting the Flood in the galaxy, were killed in the process. For whatever reason, they had felt it was necessary to contain and study the Flood, rather than destroy them outright. Their allowance of the Flood's perpetuation and storage in stasis could be considered an inexcusable lack of foresight for such an advanced civilization, though without knowing their precise reasoning, the passing of judgment is problematic.

The Forerunner perished (or fled) some 100,000 years ago, leaving their robotic progeny behind to defend and monitor their installations: seven massive rings, dozens of orbital installations around gas giants, and extensive facilities buried beneath the strata of innumerable worlds. Their Sentinel drones are floating mantis-like machines, using what is presumably Forerunner weapon and shield technology. Unlike the Human and Covenant arsenal, the Sentinels use some sort of controlled stream of energy. Deadly and precise, they appear to be more like surgical cutting tools than offensive weaponry and, while effective against the Flood's lower forms, are easily overcome by the Warrior class. Delta Halo 05 was also home to a series of smaller Repair-class robots, as well as to the large, Enforcer-class guards.

As mentioned, the Forerunners' relics are not restricted to the Halo network. The Aztec-esque stones of C'ort Azur, the arches and weathered inscriptions of Sigma Octanus, the intricate caverns and three-kilometer-wide holographic dome beneath ONI's CASTLE complex at Reach, the ancient stepping-stones of the Grunt's homeworld, the

Prophet's own claim to have evolved on an abandoned Forerunner planet, the revelation that their Ark (whatever that entails) exists on Earth, not to mention the countless installations undoubtedly pilfered to allow the Covenant to have achieved their current levels of technology—all are testament to this galaxy's complete permeation. To add to the mystery, in addition to their own constructions, their facilities often showcase and protect buildings and structures from an earlier era that seemingly predates their own.

But who were these Forerunners; these Truth-Givers? What are the details of their relationship to the Covenant; what are they to Humanity? The Covenant, garbed in their glyphs, pay an eerie homage to those symbols depicted in the interiors of the Halos' buildings, whereas Humankind seems all too at home and recognized by the rings' Monitors. Their former presence on Earth seems but the first stirring of a maelstrom. Much remains to be answered; not long is left to wait.

The Gravemind:

"I? I am a monument to all your sins..."

Gravemind is yet another enigma. Cognizant, emotional, and cunning, he is the guiding force behind the Flood found on Delta Halo 05 and possibly beyond. It is not known if he should be referred to as "the" or "a" Flood Intelligence. whether he is a singular source and leader or a Flood form that will eventually grow under the proper conditions. It is also unknown how he manages to communicate with the other Flood, and if he possesses somewhat reasonable motives and aspirations beyond the mindless hunger the Flood has thus far been known for. He does appear to be capable of some rather impressive feats: utilizing the Halo's teleportation grid, assimilating and linking with other machinery and deceased life forms (2401 Penitent Tangent and the Prophet of Regret), and, in capturing John and the Arbiter from their respective locations, a sort of omnipresence. With the annexation of *High Charity*, its tremendous biological and technological assets, and (apparently) the willing ear of Cortana, the next move is certainly his.

Halo:

For exactly 101,217 local years, it lay forgotten and derelict in a disused portion of space. Sedentary, save for the unrelenting pull of Basis and Threshold, Halo was a testament to both the drive and technological capability of its builders. It was constructed to withstand innumerable millennia, and this superannuated edifice certainly shows that the Forerunner were very capable at their craft. And so Installation 04 sat; left derelict for eons by its makers, yet apparently benignly visited and documented by numerous other races throughout its quiescent past. Not until recently, however, was its true purpose dredged from its depths.

Upon return to Einsteinian space at the coordinates detailed upon the rune-etched rock of Sigma Octanus, Cortana and Jacob Keyes discovered the ring. Roughly 10,000 kilometers in diameter, 22.3 kilometers thick, and at least 320 kilometers wide, Halo remains in orbit at a Lagrange point between Basis, the moon, and Threshold, the gas giant (Earth Survey Catalogue Number B1008-AG). With the *Pillar of Autumn* immutably crippled and their defeat unavoidable, Keyes decided to abandon ship and take flight to Halo.

Halo's geography was much like they had hoped, but far from what they could have expected. It was Earth-like, complete with mountains, hills, plains, seas, rivers, waterfalls, swamps, deserts, and icy canyons, with the only surprise being just how multi-climatic it was, considering that Halo was artificial. At a cursory glance, it seemed to be little more than a large and habitable ring-shaped construct; a feat of engineering and will. But, as they delved further into the interiors of Halo, and as they continued to monitor Covenant transmissions, they began to suspect that Halo was more than a mere ecosystem. The almost termitic passageways and arcane machinery of the Forerunner were intricately woven throughout the entire structure. And although Halo outwardly appeared to be benign, its seemingly contradictory purpose was soon discovered.

When Cortana uploaded herself into Halo's network, she uncovered Halo's true use, which the Covenant only had mild inferences of. Halo was designed as a laboratory to study, as a prison to contain, and as a sterilant to prevent, all to keep the Flood (a conscious, parasitic, almost meta-viral organism) from spreading from planet to planet throughout the galaxy. It was indeed a weapon, and though mysteriously it was not an all-smiting "cudgel," seemingly not one that could be accurately wielded by either Covenant or Human against each other. With a maximum individual range of 25,000 light years, the Halo network would easily destroy them both, and all other life capable of sustaining the Flood. What good it does to kill all life *quickly* before all life is merely consumed by the Flood *eventually* is known only to the builders. It appears that susceptible life situated on the ring is also eliminated.

After the Master Chief is made aware of Halo's true function, it was decided that it should be destroyed to prevent 343 Guilty Spark from finding someone else more willing or less resourceful to activate Halo at some point in the future. Amidst the Covenant cries of heresy the Master Chief and Cortana succeeded in ending the threat of Alpha Halo 04 , by blasting the vent core of the *Pillar of Autumn*. One down, six to go.

Another piece of the puzzle, Delta Halo 05 is the second of seven ancient ring facilities to be discovered by the Covenant and Humanity alike. It remains intact, though at the mercy of the Flood.

Halsey:

As the "mother" of Cortana, the SPARTAN-IIs, and project MJOLNIR, Dr. Catherine Halsey (civilian ID #10141-026-SRB4695) is quite possibly the author of Humanity's only true chance at halting the Covenant's campaign of cleansing and pillaging. Although a civilian, her work for ONI and dedication to the survival of a unified Human government and its people have earned her the highest security clearance available for non-military personnel, a restriction that has been stretched and broken innumerable times. A growing respect and budget have also ensued, much to the embarrassment and frustration of her rivals, namely Colonel Ackerson and his own mysterious special weapons program.

Her motivations have always been pure: to protect Humanity from forces both without and within. However, focusing on the necessity and positive yields of her operations, Dr. Halsey had reluctantly bought into ONI's concept of "acceptable losses," always for the greater good and preservation of the species. Her pride and satisfaction have always been coupled with a deep remorse for those she has sacrificed along the way; a remorse she had told herself she should not entertain.

And so she has repented and is now taking steps (the details known only to herself) to save not only the many, but the few. How her kidnapping of Kelly-087 and sudden departure in an ONI stealth prowler will accomplish this is yet to be seen.

Heretics:

Though the Covenant is driven by religious zeal, not all have ascribed to it. Insurrections and rebellions have happened often throughout the Covenant's long history: the Hunter problem and the Grunt Rebellion, to name a few that we are aware of.

This most recent, and most forceful, organization against the powers that be saw Elites and Grunts rallying behind another Elite, Sese 'Refumee, known more widely as the Heretic leader. As commander of an Artifact Retrieval Group investigating Threshold's Forerunner gas-mining facility, he and his compatriots were fortunate enough to be spared their brethren's fate on the ring. Spurred by information volunteered by the rescued 343 Guilty Spark, the faction renounced the Covenant's Oaths in the wake of Halo 04's destruction, initiated their plan, and set up their base on the Forerunner station and lab (which predates Halo 04 by several thousand years). It is from this station that he intended to spread his message of rebellion and enlightenment. Whether the release of the Flood on the orbital platform was accidental or merely part of his plan to "make [the Elites] see" is unknown. His death seems unnecessary now (the tragedy further augmented by the loss of the information he had accrued), and we can only hope that his onetime followers will hold no grudge against the Arbiter and rally behind the Elites left over from the now fractured Covenant.

Humans:

By the twenty-sixth century, Humans have founded a modest interstellar empire. There are at least a few dozen (but more likely one or two hundred) colony worlds within human-explored space in our little corner of the Orion Arm. Some of them, if not most, are heavily populated, indications of a prosperous two centuries exploring our neck (or arm, if you like) of the galaxy.

In 2525, contact is lost with the colony world Harvest. An investigating reconnaissance team disappears. Months later, a Human battle group finds the world razed—entirely "glassed" by the intense heat of orbital bombardment—and the only remaining enemy vessel claims two-thirds of the Human ships before it is destroyed. Decades and hundreds of skirmishes later, the routine is the same: Covenant ships appear, transmit cryptic messages of zeal and destruction (in Human languages, puzzlingly), and proceed to annihilate the world. Though Human forces eventually grow adept, even confident, in ground engagements (when the opportunity arises), they simply cannot claim victory in orbit. The inevitable outcome is as sickening as it is familiar.

Human technology is not that far advanced from what we have today; the basic technologies are mostly the same, but on a larger scale, with the exception of FTL travel made possible by the Shaw-Fujikawa slipstream drives of Human starships. Weaponry is still projectile-based, and explosives still seem to involve chemical reactions rather than a release of contained "plasma" or energy. While Humans have recently come to possess artificial gravity (another product of reverse engineering Covenant ordnance, as demonstrated on the *Pillar of Autumn*), they have yet to apply it to smaller planet-bound vehicles; the Warthog, for example, still uses wheels and does not hover or fly (at least not without a skilled and daring driver).

AI is a different story. Mankind has long striven to artificially produce some semblance of consciousness, and its dedication has not been in vain. Though Mankind still does not understand the complexities of the human mind, it has succeeded in at least duplicating it. In Humanity's limited extraterrestrial experience, the likes of Cortana appear only to be matched, if at all, by the constructs of the ancient Forerunner themselves. Covenant AI, though inherently complicated and dangerous, prove to be little more than simple-minded curiosities to Cortana, as she so effortlessly dissects and examines her would-be tormenters.

The Covenant, however, "own nothing which they have not stolen" and have had a decisive advantage so far in their own technological revolutions, i.e., the raiding of abandoned Forerunner complexes, caches, and worlds. But, as Humanity's resistance plays out across the fields and starscapes of the Milky Way, Mankind has not only adapted and incorporated, but created and improved. The MJOLNIR armor and shield technology, coupled with the yields of Humanity's fascination with sentient constructs, has so far been the most successful of their ingenuities.

The bulk of Humanity still does not know about the events that transpired after the *Pillar of Autumn* jumped away from the Reach; the Covenant still loomed over Human space. Even with ONI's morale-boosting propaganda and hush tactics, every night the people of Earth watched the sky, waiting for the hammer to fall. They did not have to wait for long.

Jacob Keyes:

Jacob Keyes was a member of the UNSC Navy for much of his life, slowly working his way through the ranks until finally becoming a Captain in the battle of Sigma Octanus, going on to command the *Pillar of Autumn.*

At some point early in his military career, when he was still an Ensign, Keyes was nearly killed when a captain of his independently decided to try out a new method of FTL transfer and the experiment went horribly awry. Keyes learned during the trial of the captain to keep his mouth shut—a skill that Dr. Halsey, the SPARTAN-II project, and, no doubt, ONI recognized as supremely valuable. As such, Keyes was involved in the initial exfiltration of the then young Spartans-to-be, beginning with John-117, the one-day Master Chief. With Keyes's experience, it was no surprise he was chosen to lead the *Pillar of Autumn* on its SPARTAN insertion operation.

When the *Pillar of Autumn* reached Halo, Keyes was in command of what was possibly the last group of human soldiers from Reach. From what he understood, he saw that if he failed and Halo was lost to the whims of the Covenant, Reach would certainly not be the last planet to fall, and Earth's imminent discovery and siege would be hastened exponentially. When an already dismal situation degraded even further, only his steadfast will and resolve prevented Earth from falling into the hands of a foe more threatening than even the Covenant: the omni-parasitic, sentient xenoform known as The Flood. His interrogation and eventual death by the parasite, though slow and horrific, was consistently fought with the courage and tactical skill his life and command had become known for.

Johnson:

The Man. The Myth. The Legend.

Whatever the grizzly details of Sgt. Avery Johnson's current reputation, he has certainly earned it. And, if you have anything snarky to add, you had better be well out of boot range when you do.

Several things characterize Johnson's known career thus far: his bad-ass command style, addiction to Flip music (a descendant of old Earth "Metal"), and his apparent infection and assumed death at the hands of the Flood, as recorded on the headset of the late Pvt. Jenkins.

Unable to harmonize with and thereby commandeer his nervous system because of its erratic behavior as a symptom of Boren's Syndrome, the Flood simply passed him over. Or he fought his way out in a stunning and preternatural display of agility and strength. Or both. It all depends on who's talking.

Either way, the growing rumors surrounding his possible status as a Spartan 1.0 are not without foundation.

Unlike many other members of the Human military, Johnson holds no grudges or prejudices against "freakish" Spartans, or even Elite warriors when the situation demands it. He is motivated by a hatred for the Covenant's goals and a desire to protect his race, and he'll need all the mop-up crew he can muster to follow in his wake.

The Master Chief:

The Master Chief was the sole Spartan to leave the Reach system aboard the *Pillar of Autumn* (with the exception of Linda-058 in cryo). For all he knew, he was the last SPARTAN-II alive. All of humanity depended on him, for even after their defeat at Halo 04 the Covenant was undaunted and resolved, and there were new threats and variables to contend with of which Earth remained ignorant: the Flood, the Forerunner, and their methodical creations, such as 343 Guilty Spark.

After his whirlwind tour of Delta Halo, his introduction to a host of new allies and actors, and a hitchhike back to Earth aboard a Forerunner vessel, it remains only to be seen how the Master Chief plans on "finishing this fight."

The Master Chief has lived most of his life in various military camps on the planet Reach: stolen ("recruited") from his family at age six and his name purged and amended to John-117, his entire upbringing has been centered around making him a mechanism of pure military efficiency, able to utilize both blinding force and dazzling strategy. He displays a rare sort of attitude for such a capable creation: he does not glorify his violent actions, but merely does what he has to do. He does not hate his enemies; he kills them because he knows it is his duty to kill them: "It wasn't [the Chief's] job to make things suffer—he was just here to win battles. Whatever it took" (*The Fall of Reach* 6).

He is an unconventional hero, for though he is strong, fast, and tactically brilliant, he is the epitome of none of those attributes and is surpassed by other Spartans in each area. What he does possess above all is leadership and, to both Cortana's repeated awe and bewilderment, probability-defying luck.

Miranda Keyes:

Miranda Keyes is, as far as we know, the only surviving child of the late Captain Jacob Keyes. It is unclear how well they knew one another, though it is unquestionable that she thinks both highly and fondly of him. She has apparently risen quite quickly through the UNSC, already achieving the rank of Commander and acquiring her own vessel, the *In Amber Clad*, at a relatively young age. Like her father, she is bold, imaginative, and not likely to ask for assistance. But, also like her father, her daring and courage may yet prove to be an integral step in Humanity's salvation from the Covenant.

ONI:

Much like its acronym's literal namesake ("Oni": Japanese for an ilk of mythological dæmons), the UNSC Office of Naval Intelligence manages to simultaneously elicit both blatant awe and suspicious fear, while existing in both the forefront and shadows of Humanity's military operations. Their presence is unmistakable, but its details and internal organization are largely unknown.

Section 3 and NavSpecWep are involved in all aspects of covert and black operations, intelligence gathering, special weapons research and development (the SPARTAN-II program), mission planning, and consultation.

Section 2 of ONI is involved primarily in propaganda and data manipulation, both in the name of security and keeping the hopes of Humanity set high.

(Nothing, so far, is known about the implied Sections 1 or 0.)

ONI's people are everywhere, as demonstrated by Lieutenant Haverson, formerly (and secretly) aboard the *Pillar of Autumn* and rescued from the wreckage of Halo 04. Although compliant and dedicated, most operatives have a tendency to act above the law, often skirting their own protocols for the sake of speed, subtlety, and effectiveness. They have sacrificed whole worlds for mere intel, and may be involved in plots and compromises not guessed at by even the most conspiracy-minded individual. Thankfully, while they may tempt fate and hoard their secrets, Humanity's preservation is still a top (well, at least relatively high) priority.

Prophets:

Once locked in a bitter war with the Elites, the discovery of Forerunner technology quelled hostilities long enough to form a pact where the Elites would protect the Prophets and facilitate the ransacking of the galaxy in a joint attempt to discover the mode of the Forerunner's ascension from physical reality (what they refer to as the Great Journey). Though formed through mutual agreement and governed by a Council of both races, the three High Prophets known as the Hierarchs (most recently the Prophets of Truth, Mercy, and Regret) ultimately control all aspects of the Covenant's government, theology, and military. Whether their understanding and claim to have evolved on a planet laden with Forerunner tech or their intrinsic skill at manipulation has secured their place as the Covenant priest-leaders is not fully known. Regardless, the Prophets are by far the most subtle, mysterious, guileful, and possibly vengeful of the Covenant races.

The SPARTAN-II Project:

The modern SPARTAN programs (in contrast to their ancient Greek counterpart) were initiated in 2491, as an element of the ORION project. Though not much is known about the first generation of warriors (their training, augmentation, goals, etc.)—other than that they were recruited from the best of the military's ranks—they were successful enough to garner the necessary consent for a second phase, aptly named SPARTAN-II. Under Dr. Halsey, the Spartans would be developed in conjunction with the MJOLNIR armor project, the successful culmination of a powered exoskeleton technology that had been used for some time by the UNSC (not always with positive feedback), and, when understandably discarded, by frustrated cargo handlers everywhere. The initial goal of the SPARTAN/MJOLNIR project was to provide a surgical strike team capable of dealing with Human rebellions quickly and efficiently, averting the use of large-scale military force, and preventing the civil war, and tremendous loss of life, that would have inevitably ensued with the progression of the current political climate.

Out of 150 surveyed, a total of seventy-five children, approximately age six and selected for their specific genetic dispositions (that is, being as close to perfect as science could determine), were "recruited" (appallingly, the recruitment was entirely legal under a strict reading of an otherwise uninteresting and benign piece of legislation). They were replaced with congenitally defective flash-clones to cover the enlistment and trained, primarily on and below the surface of Reach, by one Chief Petty Officer Mendez, arguably the best drill instructor in the Navy. Their family names, whatever they may have been, were stripped, purged from record, and forever replaced with a three-digit designation. Their upbringing would be defined not only by grueling physical routine, but by a comprehensive academic tutelage under Deja, a Class II AI created specifically for the SPARTAN-II project (a sign of its immense importance).

In March of 2525, on the orbital ONI Medical Facility above Reach, the then-fourteen-year-old candidates underwent a series of drastic and inadvisable operations to dramatically enhance their skeletal, muscular, optical, and nervous systems. Of the original seventy-five, only thirty-three reportedly survived the processes; thirty were lost, and twelve irrevocably crippled (though still used by ONI in research and ops planning). Indomitable previously, they were nigh-invincible afterwards.

Both before and after their final union with the MJOLNIR armor, the SPARTAN-IIs—with their overwhelming physical abilities, improvisational skills, and keenness for adversity and challenge—handled their operations with a profound efficiency: as of August 27, 2552, they had suffered only three KIAs and one too wounded to continue active duty, giving them the best record of any UNSC unit. Of course, any casualties were officially listed as only MIA, part of ONI Section 2's successful propaganda campaign to boost morale in the military's ranks, a propaganda program spearheaded by the SPARTAN-IIs and their glorious triumphs in innumerable battles, though predictably silent concerning Humanity's slow and imminent loss of the war against the Covenant.

Their existence no longer a closely guarded secret, the SPARTAN-IIs have recently added "poster child" to their official job description; they have become faceless faces of hope. However, despite their phenomenal effectiveness in terms of both military efforts and morale-building, they have proven too valuable, indeed irreplaceable, given the costs of time and energy necessary to create them: "They Can Do The Impossible"™, but cannot be squandered to achieve it.

Hence, although it has long been assumed that future classes of SPARTAN-IIs have been trained in secret, in reality the program has been discontinued. However, it has spawned an even more covert group of special forces, unknown even to their predecessors, the SPARTAN-IIIs: young, mass-produced, cheaply armored, hastily trained, yet augmented within a hair's breadth (or to a misguided stumble over) of ethical and moral boundaries. These troops are deployed in high-risk theaters and operations with a low probability of successful extraction, a.k.a. suicide missions. The public would never approve to batches of 300 children being abducted, trained, and thrust into the maws of death while only weeks beyond a chemically induced puberty, but thanks to the complete secrecy and ultimate efficacy of the program, what they don't know has done more than its share of keeping things from hurting them.

Since the SPARTAN-IIs' harrowing escape from Reach and the destruction of nearly 500 Covenant vessels consumed in the explosion of the Covenant Command Station *Unyielding Hierophant*, the arduous task of defending Humanity from the still gargantuan Covenant fleet (wise to the Earth's location) fell into the Spartans' "big, green, armored hands." Though their numbers were bolstered to seven (or eight, including the abducted Kelly) before their return to Earth, the story's continuation so far focuses solely on SPARTAN-117. Let us hope that one is enough.

Spec-Ops Commander:

Somber and professional, the high-ranking Spec-Ops Elite Rtas 'Vadumee (nicknamed "Half-Jaw" for loss of a mandible) leads his troops into battle with a rare care and sensibility. He has been through a great deal, from quelling heresy to skirmishes with the Flood, but will find his greatest challenge yet as he fights against the betrayal and attempted annihilation of his race by the Prophets and Brutes.

Tartarus:

Tartarus is the lowest depths of the Earth—the realm of the dead—and, in our case, the Chieftain of the Brutes. The Brutes are the most recent annexation of the Covenant and appear to be one of its most zealous members. Their affinity for violence, their "brute" strength, and their unquestionable dedication to the Prophets have made them the favored race of the Hierarchs. While Truth may hide some motive for replacing the Elites, Tartarus and his company are lead by a pure desire to usurp them and become the Prophet's honored escort on the Great Journey. Tartarus schemed to acquire power and a place for himself in this "salvation," but even his mighty hammer, the "Fist of Rukt," could not deliver him; at his death at the hands of the Arbiter, he remained only a blind pawn.

UNSC:

The faces of United Nations Space Command are varied—the Keyes family, Marines, Orbital Drop Shock Troopers (ODST Helljumpers), Foehammer, Lord Hood—but their goal of defending Humanity has always been the same. The UNSC military forces have suffered incredible losses at the hands of the Covenant's precise and lethal prowess. Faring best on the ground but hopelessly outnumbered and outgunned in space, the UNSC has nonetheless slowed the Covenant's advance long enough to demonstrate again and again the superior ingenuity of Humanity at large. Whether it be artificial gravity, shield technology, MJOLNIR armor—with time these already staggering advancements could be improved upon exponentially, potentially allowing the UNSC to turn the tables.

Time, unfortunately, is not something Humanity has an excess of.

Fatigued and thinly spread, the remaining forces of the once colossal United Nations Space Command must regroup and prepare for the daunting task of defending and liberating the Earth from the Covenant onslaught. Though encouraged by the repulsion of Regret's small fleet, if the fall of Reach has demonstrated anything, it is that their chances of victory against a dedicated (and now occupying) force at Earth are miniscule. At an incredible price, their only hope may be to buy time for those who can more deftly assure it.

Daniel Barbour is co-editor and maintainer of Halo.Bungie.Org's *Halo Story Page*; he works as a writer and editor, spends an equal if not greater time hobbying at the same, and is currently in the final, fatigued stumbles of an oft postponed philosophy and English double major. Barbour hails from Seven Persons, Alberta, and lives a life of contrasts: striving to learn the Means Simplistic, yet invariably turning his head to catch each flashing and zapping that electric modernity has to offer. Daniel and his wife, Renae, enjoy taking time to garden, make soap, and (to an increasingly questionable extent) continue renovations in their (increasingly less decrepit) 1910 coal mansion.

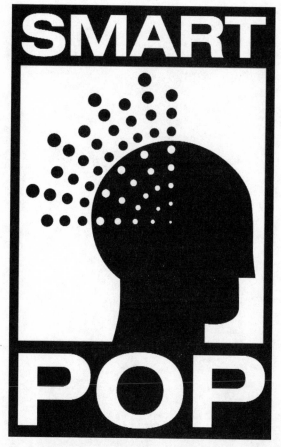

SMART POP CULTURE
SMART POP BOOKS
smartpopbooks.com

Aimed at dedicated fans of the role-playing game *World of Warcraft*, this dynamic collection of essays explores the undying fascination with a game that is a welcome escape from reality for millions of people around the world. Gaming experts, developers, and bestselling sci-fi authors examine the overwhelming success of the game and the underlying motivations for gamers to spend, on average, the time equivalent to working a part-time job battling in the world of Azeroth, and address issues ranging from economics and psychology to addiction and game ethics. The outstanding design of the game and the histories of several main characters are also discussed.

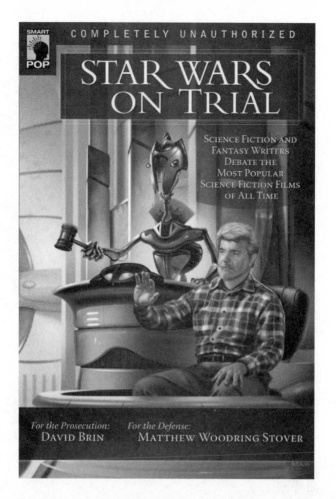

Debates on the authenticity of the Star Wars franchise and the hero-or-villain status of George Lucas are at the heart of these essays by bestselling science-fiction authors. The incredible popularity of the movies has led to the formation of strong emotions within the science fiction community on the strengths and flaws of the film, exemplified here by David Brin's attacks and Matthew Woodring Stover's defense of the movies. This intense examination of the epic works addresses a broad range of issues—from politics, religion, and the saga's overall logic to the impact of the series on bookshelf space as well as science-fiction film. The question *Is George Lucas a hero for bringing science fiction to a mass audience or a villain who doesn't understand the genre he's working for?* is discussed before a final "Judge's Verdict" on the greatness—or weakness—of the franchise is reached.

More from BenBella Books Smart Pop Series

Trekkies and Trekkers alike will get starry-eyed over this eclectic mix of essays on the groundbreaking original Star Trek series. Star Trek writers D. C. Fontana and David Gerrold, science fiction authors such as Howard Weinstein, and various academics share behind-the-scenes anecdotes, discuss the show's enduring appeal and influence, and examine some of the classic features of the show, including Spock's irrationality, Scotty's pessimism, and the lack of seatbelts on the Enterprise. The impact of the cultural phenomenon on subsequent science-fiction television programs is explored, as well as how the show laid the foundation for the science fiction genre to break into the television medium.

smartpopbooks.com | BenBella Books

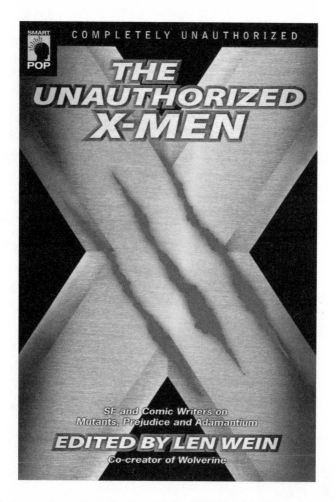

Science Fiction and comic writers trace the X-Men series' evolution, challenge its metaphors, and draw from its truths about human nature and human society in this exploratory look at the still-timely and often-revamped classic. With such essays as "Magneto the Jew," "The New Mutants and the Corruption of the Teenager" and "The Sexuality of X-Men," the contributors highlight the strange ties between the characters and current society. From mutant subcultures in the real world to the reality of racism and heterosexism not so different from that of the world of the X-Men, this book takes on the intersection between fiction and truth in a manner perfect for long-time comic readers, cartoon fans and Johnny-come-lately moviegoers.